To Karen

Sarah
of the Border Wars

---

by James D. Yoder

Every good wish
James D Yoder
9/18/04

Newton, Kansas

Other Faith & Life Press books
by James D. Yoder

The Yoder Outsiders

Barbara: Sarah's Legacy

Sarah of the Border Wars

Copyright © 1993 by Faith & Life Press, Newton, Kansas 67114-0347. This publication may not be reproduced, stored in a retrieval system, or transmitted in whole or in part, in any form by any means, electronic, mechanical, photocopying, recording, or otherwise without prior permission of Faith & Life Press.

Printed in the United States of America

96 95 94 93 4 3 2 1

Library of Congress Number 93-72125

International Standard Book Number 0-87303-213-6

This is a work of fiction built around historical events; any similarities to persons presently living is coincidental.

Editorial direction for Faith & Life Press by Susan E. Janzen; copyediting by Edna Krueger Dyck; design by John Hiebert; printing by Mennonite Press. Cover art by Joy Dunn Keenan.

DEDICATION

To the memory of Elwanda Smith, a Mennonite sister and member of Rainbow Mennonite Church, Kansas City, Kansas, who stirred our spirits by her soul-moving renditions of the hymns and songs of slaves.

A NOTE FROM THE AUTHOR

Is this historical fiction a true story? The answer is both yes and no.

There were people named Sarah and Solomon Yoder who moved from Ohio to Missouri in 1860. The first chapters are based upon records and historical accounts listed in the credits. In addition, many of the early details were narrated to me by Nona Yoder of Cass County, Missouri, when she was ninety-three years old. Nona was the granddaughter of Sarah and Solomon Yoder.

Solomon was forced to enter the Union Army against his wishes, and Sarah did live with a black woman for awhile. They had a daughter named Nancy who died soon after the Rebel bushwhacker raid upon their house.

Much of the account of the tragic affairs leading up to the Quantrill raids, including the one on Lawrence, Kansas, are based on actual happenings. Records indicate that approximately 150 Quantrill sympathizers rode on horseback very near the Yoder farm to join the raid on Lawrence.

Following the raid on Lawrence and the issuance of "Order Number Eleven," the Yoders fled back to Ohio. They were led by Solomon's brother, C.P. Yoder.

Later, the Yoders returned to Missouri, moving farther eastward in Cass County. Readers who know something of the history of the Mennonite communities of Cass County will recognize that at this point I have blended two Yoder families into one for my story line, and the book is fictionalized.

There was a Barb Yoder who had a sister named Salome. They became the famous Yoder sisters, managing their well-kept farmstead. On plot maps of the period, their farm is marked "The Yoder Sisters." As a child during the Depression years, we moved to this "Barb Yoder Place." Once a prestigious farm with fine buildings, it was then in serious decline. Readers may read of this decline and many of my childhood events on the Barb Yoder place in my book, *The Yoder Outsiders* (Newton, Kans.: Faith and Life Press, 1988). Though the buildings were in decline, the wonderful trees and creeks were still there offering their grace and healing—even the paw paw bushes and blackberries and gooseberries noted in this book. I recall selling gooseberries that I picked from those woods to old Barb Yoder, and I recall her telling me that she remembered when Abraham Lincoln was president. Yes, it is a true story in the sense that it reflects much of the history of the time, as well as the themes radiating from the lives of these near frontier Mennonites.

James D. Yoder

ACKNOWLEDGEMENTS

Numerous people shared stories with me from time to time, some in formal interviews, many in informal periods and visits through the years. Though I probably cannot name them all, I particularly thank the following for their sharing and help in making this story possible: Mary Kathryn Yoder, Nona Yoder (deceased), Nellie Roth (deceased), Ida Hershberger (deceased), Reuben Yoder (deceased) and Ruth Yoder, and Lorene Roth, all of Harrisonville, Missouri; Nellie King, Garden City, Missouri; Mary King and Sadie King Yoder, Kalona, Iowa; Elwanda Smith (deceased), Kansas City, Kansas; Ernst Penner, Newton, Kansas; Alma Mast, Sanford and Berta Miller, Christina Garber, Elsie White, Iona and Wilbur Schrock (formerly of Garden City, Missouri), all of Hesston, Kansas; Ruby Zook and Ira Zook (deceased), Goshen, Indiana; Neva White, Manhattan, Kansas.

CREDITS

Chapter 1 The hymn, "My Soul with Humble Fervor Raise," by Livingston, 1789, is from the *Lieder und Melodienbuch* (Elkhart, Ind.: Mennonite Publishing House, 1895).

Chapter 2 References to pre-Civil War conflict within the border states, including materials about the Kansas Jayhawks and Redlegs and the Southern Bushwhackers, are from *History and Directory of Cass County,* published by the Cass County Leader (Harrisonville, Mo., 1908). The book was loaned to the author by Mary Kathryn Yoder of Harrisonville, Missouri.

Other references to border war conflicts and Civil War battles also come from the booklet, *Decade of Decision, 1855-1865,* edited by Robert S. Townsend (Kansas City Life Insurance Company, 1960).

Chapter 3 The military orders are found in *History and Directory of Cass County,* Cass County *Leader* (Harrisonville, Mo., 1908).

Chapter 4 The hymn, "O Love Divine," by J. Claude Brunk is from *The Church and Sunday School Hymnal with Supplement* (Scottdale, Pa.: Mennonite Publishing House, 1902). Used by permission.

Chapter 6 Accounts regarding Sarah Yoder residing with a former slave woman around 1860-1863 were told to me by the granddaughter of Sarah and Solomon Yoder, Nona Yoder, now deceased, of Harrisonville, Missouri, in an interview in March 1990.

Chapter 7 The quotation from Stonewall Jackson is from *War, Peace and Nonresistance* by Guy F. Hershberger (Scottdale, Pa.: Herald Press, 1946), p. 108. Used by permission.

Chapter 12 The story of the battle near St. Thomas Wharf, Waverly, Missouri, and the large wooden gun is told in *Decade of Decision, 1855-1865,* edited by Robert S. Townsend (Kansas City, Mo.: Kansas City Life Insurance Company, 1960).

Chapter 13 The story of the two Anabaptist girls is from *The Bloody Theatre or Martyrs Mirror* by T.J. van Braght (Scottdale, Pa.: Herald Press, 1950), p. 501.

Chapter 15 The account of the plundering of Sarah Yoder's house and removing of the bed clothing from Nancy's bed was told to me by Nona Yoder, a niece of the deceased Nancy Yoder.

Chapter 16 The Negro spiritual lyrics were given to me by Elwanda Smith, a member of the Rainbow Mennonite Church, Kansas City, Kansas. They represent songs of the times and the songs of slaves. The text of "Children of the Heav'nly Father" is copyrighted by the Board of Publication, Lutheran Church in America. Reprinted by permission of Augsburg Fortress.

Chapter 17 Accounts of events that led up to the issuance of "Order Number Eleven" were from notebooks and clippings from the *Cass County Democrat,* loaned to me by Mary Kathryn Yoder, and from *The History of the Mennonite*

Settlement in Cass County, Missouri by Iona Schrock, a member of the Sycamore Grove Mennonite Church. These accounts, as well as a copy of "Order Number Eleven" issued by General Euwing, were loaned by the Mid-Continent Library of Jackson County in Independence, Missouri. Accounts of the Quantrill raid are also based on stories recorded in *History and Directory of Cass County* (Harrisonville, Mo.: Cass County Leader, 1908), and *Centennial History of Missouri V. 1,* by Walter Stevens (St. Louis: S. J. Clarke Publishing Co., 1921), pp. 684-85.

The quote from Bingham in the *Washington Sentinal is* found in *History and Directory of Cass County* (Harrisonville, Mo.: Cass County *Leader,* 1908), pp. 124ff.

Chapter 20 The stories of Sarah Yoder trying to find seclusion at Ft. Harrisonville were told to the author on March 9, 1990, by her granddaughter, Nona Yoder, of Harrisonville, Missouri. Accounts of Sarah and Solomon Yoder are also recorded in *History of Cass County* by Allen Glenn (Topeka and Cleveland: Historical Publishing Co., 1917), p. 629.

The Bingham quote is from *History and Directory of Cass County* (Harrisonville, Mo.: Cass County *Leader,* 1908), p. 132.

A letter from J.D. Hartzler, formerly of Cass County, Missouri, dated April 16, 1946, to Melvin Gingerich, tells briefly of some of Sarah and Solomon Yoder's trials and the memories of the events of Barbara Yoder Blank. The letter is now property of Mennonite Historical Society, Goshen, Indiana.

Chapter 22 "O Love Divine" by J. Claude Brunk is from *The Church and Sunday School Hymnal with Supplement* (Scottdale, Pa.: Mennonite Publishing House, 1902). Used by permission.

Chapter 23 The account of the swarms of grasshoppers in Cass County and surrounding areas is recorded in *The History of Missouri, V. II,* by David March (New York: Lewis Historical

Publishing Co., 1967), pp. 1056-1057.

Chapter 25 The author lived on the Barb Yoder place for nine years when he was a child. He remembers the thousands of gooseberry bushes, blackberries, many kinds of hickory nuts, walnuts, and hazelnuts in the woods along Camp Branch. Even in the 1940s, many persons from surrounding farms came to pick nuts and berries. The account of Bishop Jake Kanagy and his dressing up for the conservative Mennonites from the East is recorded in *South Central Frontiers* by Paul Erb (Scottdale, Pa.: Herald Press, 1974), p. 82.

Chapter 28 Stanzas from the hymn "Tread Softly," words by Fanny J. Crosby, are from *Church Hymnal* (Scottdale, Pa.: Mennonite Publishing House, 1927). Used by permission.

German translations of Scripture by Ernst Penner of Newton, Kansas; also "Gott Ist Die Liebe" in *Church and Sunday School Hymnal* (Scottdale, Pa.: Mennonite Publishing House, 1902). Used by permission.

Chapter 29 Materials relating to Mennonite farms and farmers of Cass County are mentioned in *History of Cass County* by Allen Glenn. Also township plot maps showing the farms and names of the Mennonite owners were found at the Mid-Continent Library, Independence, Missouri.

Chapter 30 The poem, "Don't Thee Wed," was found in *The History of Missouri, V. II,* by David March (New York: Lewis Historical Publishing Company, 1967), p. 395. It is a poem of the 1880s.

Chapter 33 Matthew 25:34-40 is quoted from *The Holy Bible,* Authorized King James Version (London, New York and Toronto: Oxford University Press). Other Bible passages are from the same translation.

Chapter 1

Sarah King Yoder raised her aching body from the sweet, warm soil in her spring garden. Resting her left hand against the small of her back, she brushed a few wisps of dark hair out of her eyes with her bronzed fingers. She surveyed the scene before her.

It was a good land, this Missouri. Sarah whispered the word softly, dragging the vowels as she breathed it. She smiled and her red lips gleamed from the intoxication of the spring air and the young blood surging through her body.

Missouri. The word slipped from her lips like the soughing of the west wind through the giant cedars in her front yard. Her eyes focused ahead upon her tanned husband, Solomon, plowing the lower twenty acres. His black mules strained as they pulled the walking plow through the rich soil of the Grand River bottoms.

Solomon. Sarah loved to breathe the name of her tall husband and she never tired of looking at him. When he stepped back from his plow and stood straight, his lean body raised to just over six feet. Heaving crowbars against resisting stumps had broadened his back and strengthened his shoulders.

Solomon trimmed his red-brown beard a little. Shaved to avoid any military look, his upper lip often curled in tune with a twinkling eye as he chuckled or whirled Sarah in an old Virginia reel. Solomon Yoder was a handsome man, but

Mennonites were not, of course, among those who spoke of men as handsome or women as pretty. Weren't all people precious and wonderful in God's sight?

Sarah chuckled as Solomon struggled with his mules who'd stopped to graze the lush sour dock and fennel growing by the rail fence edge.

"Mother?" Nancy turned and asked, "Why are you laughing?"

"Chuckling at your father, child. I know how upset he gets when those mules start balking."

She smiled at the fair-haired child. What would life be like in this troubled land without a child? Only ten years old, the child could pick peas and shell them just as fast as she. This week she planned to teach Nancy how to knead bread dough. But, would her young arms be strong enough for the job? This gentle child who wanted to do the work of a frontier adult seemed caught between heaven and earth. A soft breeze caught Nancy's flaxen hair.

The child nearly kept up with them, and was stronger than she looked. They were a family in this new land. When they lit the candles at evening and broke the homemade bread, it was broken under the murmured blessing from the lips of Solomon's bowed head. Love hovered in their hearts and around their table.

But lately, Sarah was not always smiling. She straightened again, her tin bucket running over with the fresh peas. No, today as her eyes scanned the western horizon, she saw no clouds of dust from bands of roving jayhawkers thundering out of Kansas Territory onto this Missouri soil. She'd hold her fear—let the bliss of spring purge her soul of fear. Let God, who willed this spring, free her soul from any "arrow that flieth by day."

Sarah's homespun dress flapped about her lean thighs, revealing her sturdy form. She was glad she was thin and tall. Glad too that energy flowed through her, and the backbreaking tasks of near frontier farming in May of 1860 challenged her.

Even if her bones did ache when she lay down with Solomon upon their cornhusk mattress at night, she could smile and rest in the peace of the accomplishments of her labors.

She started to hum. Singing helped her forget the terrors lurking at the edge of her heart. She hummed an old song she'd learned back in Ohio. Yes, let the Missouri earth, verdant with spring, and the sweet air hear the old hymn from the *Lieder und Melodien:*

> My soul with humble fervor raise
> To God the voice of grateful praise
> And all my ransomed powers combine
> To bless his attributes divine.

She and Solomon brought their church with them, nurtured in their hearts, for did not the Scriptures instruct them in their duties of remembering the holy ways, "...and shalt talk of them when thou sittest in thine house, and when thou walkest by the way...."

Here and there, scattered beyond the hill, just east of Harrisonville was a small sprinkling of Old Order Amish, Dunkers, and three or four families from their own Ohio Mennonite tradition.

Crowded eastern communities and the cheaper, yet fertile, land had beckoned them westward. They had no meetinghouse yet, but give them time.

Sarah turned, holding her bucket of peas. She glanced once more over toward the woods and the river and her plowing Solomon. Great white-barked sycamores and towering poplars grew along the river beyond their land. Against these giants rose the red and white oak and shagbark hickory. These were edged by stands of curly leaf dogwood, clumps of elderberries and shimmering willows.

One could sit on a stump and feast on such sights half a morning. Windswept clouds cast fleeting shadows over the green pasture and black sod. Hundreds of songbirds rejoiced in Mother Nature's heady burst of spring.

She called back toward the garden, "Nancy, when your pail is full, bring it around to the back porch." They'd shell the peas together. She'd stew some for noon dinner. She already had a chunk of smoked ham roasting in the oven. Now, she needed to get her bread baked.

Before Sarah closed the screen door, she looked southeastward, over to the town of Harrisonville, looming on the hill. The town was sheltered, set in among the oaks, lindens, hackberries, and hickories.

She set her pail down and sauntered over to the stone well, tipped the cedar bucket, and allowed the cool water to splash down on her calloused feet. The soil melted and slipped off her ankles and toes, sinking into the earth.

When the sun had reached its height for the day, Solomon, beard and hair blowing in the wind, had already tied his team of mules by the mulberry tree on the other side of the well.

The mules, Old Hard and Cracklin, dipped their velvet muzzles into a cedar tub, savoring the cold water. He left a generous scoop of oats in the trough for them. Their tails slapped and flicked away the buzzing flies.

Solomon was not as lighthearted lately as was his wife. These were troublesome times. Clouds of war loomed on the horizon. Back in Ohio things were more clear-cut. Anyone could see that Ohio was the North.

Here it was as if they were in no-man's-land. He hadn't known that it would be like this. The land, the farm, the country suited Solomon fine. But Missouri was a border state. Was it North or South? There were slaveholders up on the hill at Harrisonville, east and south in Butler, Nevada, and Carthage.

Even fifty miles north on the great muddy Missouri, gentlemen farmers and well-to-do Southerners had settled, erecting huge mansions of red brick along the great river. Miles of hemp fields stretched out along the river bottoms. Slave quarters hunched among giant hardwood trees behind these mansions near Liberty and Lexington and as far east as Waverly. One in ten persons in Missouri Territory in 1860 was a slave.

Why, even Nancy and Sarah had befriended that lonely old Negro slave woman, Marianne, up in that forlorn three-story brick house of Colonel Mansfred's up on the hill.

Blood-chilling stories echoed in his ears. Stories of cutthroats and murderers who roamed the border from Kansas Territory back through these parts, Cass and Bates counties, had been circulating. These vagabonds lived by no law.

He could tell that Sarah was aware of the tension in the air. He hoped to keep the worst of such news from Nancy, though. Their child must not lie down at night and worry sleeplessly over tales of war and threats of plunder.

Two weeks past they'd met for worship, this motley little group of Anabaptists, Dunkers, Amish Mennonites, and others. They were few in number and met only once a month for religious services at Eli Zook's farm. Joseph Eicher, an ordained deacon of the Amish Mennonites, led in prayer and preached the sermon, urging them to recall their history as peace-loving, gentle, and simple people of the land.

Joseph's words, spoken in German, urged them to look upon Jesus, the author and finisher of their faith, and to remember the words of our Savior, "Those who use the sword, perish with the sword."

Joseph knew that our gentle Savior died as a slave, stretched out upon a cross, urging us to pray for our enemies.

After the meeting they visited, encouraging one another. Not a single one knew with certainty what would happen to a Mennonite, or Dunker, or Quaker brother who refused to register for the draft, or, if corralled into the Union army and be called upon to fire upon his fellow citizens. They would soon be tested.

Chapter 2

After that church service and following their shared meal, the brethren strode solemnly out toward the pasture behind Brother Zook's barn. Wanting to protect the women and children from the gloomy news, they began to share the tales of plunder among themselves.

"It's the raids under Colonel Lane coming out of Kansas that stirs fear in me," said Eli Hershberger, worriedly, while kicking a clod with his boot.

"Lane has no discipline with his troops. Jenison's Redlegs are worse, turned loose to roam like wild men," responded Andrew Miller.

Solomon remembered what he'd heard at Brodie's grist mill only last Tuesday. Redlegs, followed by a pack of thirty-seven wild, cutthroat jayhawkers, had descended upon the frontier town of Independence.

Disguised in Union garb, the dreaded Quantrill and Cole Younger, Confederate sympathizers, with ravaging war cries, threw off their disguises and cut a swath of pillage and destruction through the town.

The Union soldiers had been caught off guard. Seven buildings were ransacked and burned to the ground. Sweeping eastward along the great river, the war cries of the cutthroats sent the slave owners and their slaves, as well as faithful loyalists, into cellars, caves, and timber for hiding.

Seventeen people were murdered and blooded cattle were corralled and routed back toward Kansas. In this border country, civil law courts and constitutional guarantees were suspended from 1861 until 1865. Strife between outlaw bands was continuous.

"Ten Negro slaves were taken by these jayhawkers. They were released in Kansas, but three were shot in the confusion down by Butler," stated Moses Lehman, nervously clearing his throat.

"Brethren, if ever there's a time to put our trust in God, this is it."

Only last week, news had reached Aaron Hostetler's ears that a band of pro-slavery bushwhackers from Missouri had ridden over into Kansas to Eudora. Pillaging and plundering, they killed two farmers, corralling their livestock, driving them back to Missouri along with their wives.

The women, nearly dead of terror, were thrown off the horses in the woods by the border. Then they were set loose to find their way back to their homes, which had been burned behind them.

A letter from Solomon's brother, C.P. Yoder, back in Ohio, arrived, carried by the stagecoach from Independence through Pleasant Hill, down to Harrisonville. The letter had read, "We have heard of the plight of the citizens of Missouri. Sell your sixty acres and bring Sarah and Nancy back to Ohio. We pray for you and fear for your lives."

But Solomon and Sarah had invested the sweat and energy of their bodies in this land. Their strong bodies and hearts were committed to building a community in this new, rich land. Besides, they had no money for the costly journey by coach, then train or riverboat back to Ohio.

And what about Ohio? What protection would there be in Ohio? The rumblings of war swept like black clouds from the east coast to Kansas Territory.

"God help us," was their prayer.

Then Missouri Governor Gambel appointed General Schofield to take charge of the Military District of the Border. Schofield, in turn appointed Brigadier General Thomas Euwing, Jr., in charge of this district of warring and desperate factions. Solomon and Sarah Yoder lived exactly in the middle of this district.

While Solomon cut his wheat with his weathered cradle, he prayed in earnest, "Oh God, show me what to do."

On April 12, 1861, Southern soldiers fired upon Fort Sumter, a United States military post in Charleston, South Carolina. The Civil War erupted, pouring affliction, blood, horrors, and death from the Atlantic coast to Kansas Territory.

Sarah and Solomon finally broke their silence and put their fear into words: "What about a servant of Christ who cannot take up the sword?"

Sweat drenched Solomon's back and ran down from under his straw hat over his brow and down into his beard. He swung the cradle again as the golden wheat fell into the embrace of the forked arm.

Two hundred feet back, Sarah and Nancy, also sweating in the July heat, bent their backs, gathering the wheat, binding it into bundles.

"My family. What will happen to my family? Oh, Christ, my Savior, show me; help me in this troubled land."

He'd seen the notice nailed outside the post office in Harrisonville yesterday, just as the Batesville coach rolled dangerously southward in a cloud of thick dust, on toward New Harmony. The posted document, printed in bold, black letters, read "Federal Military Act." Solomon shuddered and his blue eyes squinted while he rapidly glanced over it. "All men from ages eighteen to forty-five, required to register post haste for the draft for the Union army."

There was a Union military post around the corner, two blocks down. Clusters of men huddled outside it, some in the new uniform. The Union forces had taken the courthouse for their headquarters and command post.

From the hidden recesses of his soul, Bible verses he'd memorized as a child surfaced. Solomon swung his cradle again—the ache in his back and the cramp of his arm muscles confirmed his aliveness. The feel of the soft earth beneath his boots, the sweet smell of the fresh cut wheat—all announced that he, Solomon Yoder, belonged to the earth.

He was alive. He, a Mennonite man who'd chosen to go westward, who bore responsibility for a wife and a daughter and for this farm and even for the animals upon it, was now faced with what seemed like a high stone wall, threatening to block his way. He'd planned to build a community and a church here. Now this.

The sacred verses coursed through his mind. "But I say unto you, that ye resist not evil; but whosoever shall smite thee on thy right cheek, turn to him the other also." And "...love your enemies, bless them that curse you, do good to them that hate you...."

Nancy and Sarah left the wheat field. The sun was sliding over a western cloud bank; the golden glow of late evening shone around them.

"Time to feed the chickens." Sarah loved her chickens. Her Rhode Island Reds were fine layers and wonderful brooding hens.

"I'll go bring in the cows for father," cried Nancy. Her faded pinafore blew in the wind as she turned by the log barn and headed down the path to the pasture near the woods.

The cows too were a special blessing. Tillie, the Guernsey, gave the most milk. Thank Tillie especially for the cheese. It would be ready to cut next week. Bossy, a headstrong Jersey, generally rebuked and resisted her milker at first. You had to let her know you meant business when you squatted by her side. Then Brindle was just plain old Brindle, all white and grey and purple streaked, chewing her cud, waiting patiently to be milked.

Sarah worked even harder under stress. All of them, and many of their farm neighbors, even the townsfolk, faced uncertain futures.

She'd surprise Solomon next week with her finished cheese, yellow gold, sliding from the tin ring mold he'd made for her. He'd punched the holes with pick and hammer from the inside out so all the whey could drip out as the cheese aged.

Sarah'd followed the recipe from her grandmother Rebecca that she had brought with her from Ohio.

She'd thanked her cows as she'd finally saved six gallons, three gallons skimmed and three gallons of whole milk. Nancy had stoked up the fire on the kitchen range while Sarah set on the copper wash boiler. Pouring in the milk, it began to heat. She added rennet, salt, and coloring. They both stirred the milk, one at each end. It had to be heated without scorching or boiling.

When the temperature of the milk seemed just right, they dragged the boiler off the fire and set it out onto the back porch to cool.

While Sarah began the evening supper, Nancy swished a small green-leafed branch back and forth over the milk to keep the flies from falling in. Nobody who bit into Sarah Yoder's cheese would ever say they swallowed a fly.

Next morning they would cut through the cheese, making small squares of curds. She'd saved that old, thin butcher knife just for this. They lifted out the curds and scooped them into a heavy cotton sack, leaving the whey in the bottom of the boiler for the pigs. Sarah carried the cheese out to the cool spring house where it would hang for two days, tub under it, to drain.

Next, Sarah emptied the curds into the cheese ring, lined with a cloth. Packing them in tightly, she fitted a circular board over the top. She left it there in the spring house with the bricks bearing down on it while it aged and drained.

Then once a week for three weeks she hurried down to the spring house to take out her cheese and wash the thickening rind with vinegar water. After three weeks—ah, what wonderful cheese! Solomon would be surprised. Maybe it would lift his spirits.

But Solomon's spirits weren't lifted. By the end of the second month after the posting of that federal military act, the state militia's deputies were riding horseback across the country to corral all men between eighteen and forty-five who had not willingly shown themselves to register.

That night as Solomon lay next to Sarah on the cornhusk mattress in their little bedroom just to the side of the kitchen, he realized that he would get little sleep.

Chapter 3

The summer moon had risen, casting a shaft of light across to the small oak dresser against the east wall. Their work clothes sagged on the wire hooks mounted on the wood framing. The skirt of Sarah's faded garden dress blew in the wind coming from the open windows. White strings of her prayer covering mounted on a green vase on the dresser, blew out toward him in the breeze.

"Her covering! A symbol of prayer. Pray for us now, dear Jesus." He closed his eyes in prayer.

It was as if she could hear the murmurings of his heart. "Hush, Solomon." Sarah slipped her calloused hand under his great bronzed and even harder hand.

"We'll find a way. We must not upset Nancy. There is so much change and trouble. We must not let her see us crumbling in fear. God is our shield and buckler."

A week ago, Solomon had ridden the five miles out beyond the Kohler hill eastward to Eli Zook's farm. What had Eli heard? What were the young men from Ohio, Pennsylvania, and even in southern Virginia doing? Their church hadn't exactly been sleeping. But, basking in the relative peace and security since the great Revolutionary War, they'd grown accustomed to peace and freedom from the military draft and persecution.

"Eli Zook got word from his nephew, Aaron Hershberger, back in Virginia. Some of the young men from the churches there have gone to the mountains to hide out until the storm has passed," Solomon said as he held Sarah's warm hand.

Their dilemma was even worse. If the Virginians took up arms, it would be on the side seeking to preserve slavery. Sarah could not see her husband fleeing to the hills. Besides, there were no vast acres of mountains here in which to hide. No. Solomon generally approached things head-on, like Old Buford, their bull, who tackled head-on anything that entered the pasture gate.

"They have issued another order," said Solomon, beginning to perspire in the summer air.

It was true. Major Thomas Biggers, Commander of the Fifth Cavalry, Missouri State Militia, had issued an order commanding all citizens of the county to declare their allegiance to the Union by an oath, and if possible, fortify the state militia by posting bonds.

"We do not swear oaths of allegiance to states and nations." They whispered the words together in their fear and apprehension.

What had happened, that quiet and innocent folks of the land were now caught in such a quandary?

Only two of the Mennonite faith had finally put their hands to the pen to plead the case for those whose faith could not allow them to take up arms. These two were Samuel Coffman of Virginia and John F. Funk of Pennsylvania.

Mennonite or Quaker and Brethren young men could pay a fee of up to 400 dollars, which would hire a substitute to go in their places. This was no answer for most of these young men. How could one whose conscience told him, "Thou shalt not kill," hire another man to be thrust forward to do the awful tasks of war?

Sarah had thought of this before. She, however, knew that even if they sold their mules and cows—even the farm, Solomon would never pay another man to go to war for him.

But they were not the only ones in anguish. It was

reported in all the papers that that sad and forlorn-looking President Lincoln had also grown weary and burdened over this matter.

"We must allow for those whose consciences will not let them take up arms. If we do not, our nation cannot expect to be blessed by God."

But the terrible rumblings of war continued to take their awful toll, brother against brother. The country split: the industrial North against the agrarian South with its slaveholders. Congress could not bring a policy together that would be applied from state to state. It ended with "every man for himself."

Lately, Solomon, in desperation, thought of staying hidden in the house or barn. Or, could he work only in the back part of his fields away from the road—out of the eye of the roaming Union deputies?

Deacon Eicher, in great haste, rode the five miles up the big hill to Fort Harrisonville. He was astonished at how quickly the military air prevailed. Hurrying, he spurred his horse on out to Solomon Yoder's place. Then he warned Brother Yoder.

"They came in the night, Solomon. David Hartzler, old Sam and Nettie's son who live one farm beyond ours, was taken."

Like night raiders, the deputy marshals knew that people could not stay in the fields forever. They waited until past midnight, then burst upon the farmhouse. Dave, confused and tired, gave up. He found some clothes and allowed them to take him.

Now Solomon knew that he would no longer stay beside Sarah in their bed at night, next to her soft, warm body. For the next four nights he slept between the rows of his tall, green corn.

Chapter 4

When she heard the heavy galloping of horse hooves, Sarah raised up from her green bean bushes and turned her eyes eastward. The hoofbeats stopped. She looked up beyond the edge of her cloth sunbonnet to see a fine sorrel horse.

Her eyes lifted higher to the shiny boots of the marshal of the state militia, tightly buttoned in his navy coat. His bearded face reflected no emotion. His eyes, like grey steel, focused upon her.

"Woman, is your name Yoder?"

Sarah's heart was pounding so hard she wondered if she could stand. Somehow, as if disconnected from her stricken heart and fear-filled mind, her sturdy legs lifted her upward.

A breeze caught her blue sunbonnet, tipping it backward. It was as if the breeze blew the strength of God into her soul. Now, she stood calmly.

"Yes. Yes sir, it is. My name is Sarah Yoder."

"You have a husband, woman?" The marshal's cold steel eyes searched over the list of names on the paper in his gloved hand. A nation was breaking, men were desperate, and most had their eyes focused upon the sword.

"Yes, I have a husband, and a daughter, Nancy."

"We're not interested in you, ma'am, nor the child. We have an order for the arrest of Solomon Yoder, unless he comes forthwith."

The wind lifted the bower of wild prairie roses, sending a branch nodding over the rail fence toward Sarah.

"Where is your husband, woman?" The tall, well-dressed marshal looked tired, but his question was a command. It hung in the air like the edge of a sharp sword.

What does one do in such hour of trial? How could she betray Solomon, the man she loved; the one building this home, this farm, this community, this church, with her?

She could lie, point in the opposite direction, send the marshal on an endless chase. In the hour of trial, Peter denied that he even knew the Lord, didn't he?

Her hesitation was only for a moment—one moment in the mystery called time, when the soul plunges downwards and finds eternal strength surging up from some unknown depths.

Sarah turned. Her eyes swept the countryside, circling the barn, the woods, the faraway, tall corn in the field.

When her eyes, filled with pain, stopped momentarily, they dropped, then lifted again as they focused upon the tall form of her conscience-burdened husband, hoe over his shoulder, striding slowly forward. He'd seen the officer from a far corn row. His faded shirt billowed in the gusts of wind. Now he began to walk briskly, straightening his tired form. Solomon had made up his mind.

"He's coming, yonder." Sarah pointed, her hand shaking, as time stood still and the fearful questions about their future hung, waiting. Then her pointing arm fell, stricken as with paralysis.

"Solomon Yoder," called the marshal. His eyes softened now by the sight: one lonely mortal, a tired, near frontier farmer, his tall, sunburned wife and blue-eyed child. Now, the marshal too felt the anguish and tragedy of war.

"You are to report to the commanding officer at Fort Harrisonville and be processed for service in the state militia for the Union army."

Sarah had never seen such anguish in Solomon's eyes. She knew that deep inside his soul the battle raged. Her heart nearly stopped as her ears caught her husband's words.

"I will report to the commander," Solomon replied evenly, feet steady beneath him. His tired eyes focused into the steel blue of the officer's eyes. "I need a day to put my things in order."

Mercifully, the officer replied, "You have until tomorrow noon. You know the alternative if you don't report?"

Yes, Solomon knew. Both deserters and runaways were shot when they were found.

It took Solomon a full day to put his farm in order. Sarah did not weep in his presence. She baked fresh bread and cut and wrapped generous wedges of her cheese, putting it on one side of his knapsack and warm, hand-knitted socks on the other.

There were no outward tears, but they flowed inwardly, coursing down over her wounded spirit. What was the answer? What should she, Sarah, do in Solomon's place with the breakdown of law—the very country crumbling, breaking apart beneath their feet?

> There shall no evil befall thee, neither shall any plague come nigh thy dwelling, for he shall give his angels charge over thee, to keep thee in all thy ways.

She'd memorized these verses when she was but a girl, reciting them from the blessed Psalms as she brought in the cattle. Oh, precious holy words! How can one live without their soul-quenching freshness?

Solomon tried to restrain his varied and throbbing emotions. His voice wavered, but did not break, as he read from Psalm 91: "He that dwelleth in the secret place of the most High shall abide under the shadow of the Almighty."

Nancy, pale with apprehension, wisps of her blond hair

blowing in the breeze from the open window, listened intensely to the holy words of comfort. Tears streaked the pale child's cheeks. Openly, the tears ran as she reached out and took her father's calloused hand.

Sarah knew that no matter what the winds of war bore, she must try to dwell in this secret place.

And she hummed. Yes, hummed to keep in time and rhythm with her breaking heart. She sang, looking with an inner eye to Jesus, that man of sorrows, the one acquainted with grief.

> O love divine that stooped to share
> Our sharpest pang, our bitt'rest tear,
> On thee we cast each earth-born care,
> We smile at pain while thou art near.

But she could not smile at this pain, deep, deep within.

She had to admit to herself as she'd kissed Solomon at that awful parting all soldiers must endure, that she felt and shared the same guilt he bore. It had been no time for smiles. It was a time of fear and a time for faith, faith from the hearts of trembling mortals.

Chapter 5

The heavy ache in Sarah's heart had not subsided. She knew she had to calm her fear for Nancy's sake. Solomon had been gone three months now. Since that day the burning smoke clouds from the battle of Morristown had risen in the west and blown over her farm with the smells of gunpowder and burning fields.

Poor pitiful souls loyal to the South found themselves hounded, chased, imprisoned, and even killed at the Union orders. She'd seen such an order herself, posted by the door of Brodie's Mill: "Order Three. Lieutenant Wilson of Company One will take twenty men and proceed in an easterly direction and capture, if possible, a carriage containing some rebel women."

If Southern women were subject to arrest, so was she, Sarah Yoder, subject to the pillaging of her farm and her life imperiled by the foraging bands of rebel soldiers and guerrilla bushwhackers.

Many of the young men from Jackson, Cass, and Butler counties had joined the rebel forces. Nancy and Sarah were caught in the crossroads of the border battles of the Civil War.

Sarah was comforted some, however, by the thought of old Mack Sherman, the broken, withered-looking field hand Solomon had insisted on hiring before he'd left. Sarah had argued that since she was a strong woman, she'd make do by herself.

She hadn't protested enough, though. She knew that Solomon's heart would be eased by the presence of Mack Sherman, a veteran of the Indian wars. He now slept in Nancy's room and Nancy shared her mother's bedroom. Sarah hated the way old Mack chewed and spit his tobacco juice, but she had to admit, his presence greatly allayed their fears.

One day, sixty-nine-year-old Mack Sherman was accosted by a band of rebel soldiers as he was taking a wagon of Sarah's grain up the winding road to Fort Harrisonville to the mill.

Mack Sherman had fallen asleep, rocking on the spring wagon seat on the journey home. The grey-clothed rebel trio had crept up silently, then two raced ahead of him as Mack's head nodded.

"Hold there!" Commanding voices challenged him and jarred him out of his reveries.

"Oh, God almighty, help me!"

Poor old Mack Sherman had thrown down the reins and was trying to leap from his wagon, but his pants had caught on the brake handle.

"Don't shoot! I'm an old man. I don't know much about this here North and South business. Don't shoot!"

Well, mercy prevailed. The rebel soldiers, youthful and intoxicated by the false wine of war, mocked him, digging at his bony ribs with their rifle barrels.

"Old man, I'll bet ya'll a goin' home to yer Indian woman, ain't you!"

They taunted him. His eyes rolled in fear. He needed a heavy draught from his friendly jug of apple jack to propel him out of this agony.

So the rebels hounded and shamed and mocked the broken old man. They'd stolen the mules, wagon, grain, and all. Their hooting taunts drifted backward as old Mack Sherman stumbled for the ditch and the cover of a stand of willows. His worn boots danced high in the air as the bullets pinged and sang at their manure-coated soles.

Their callous hooting and awful insults called back to him, pelted his soul, and seared his ego. They fired again at poor, petrified Mack Sherman. But his life was spared as Sarah's mules, Old Hard and Cracklin, and her wagon and load of grain raced off to join the rebel forces.

Chapter 6

Sarah looked over westward toward the towering trees and massive three-story brick house. "Wonder what's happened to old Marianne?" she thought.

Sarah and Nancy had bumped into Marianne at the grist mill. The old slave woman had brought in two sacks of wheat and one of corn to be ground. Her little spring wagon and tired horse were tied by the water trough.

The colonel's handsome horses had all been corralled and ridden off to war. Now no man lifted the heavy sacks for Marianne. She had been a slave all of her sixty-three years, and she did her slave work now.

She faltered, trying to lift the bulging sack of wheat out of the back of her wagon. It hit the ground with a soft thud, then tipped, tearing open. Precious grain began to spill out.

"Let us help you." Sarah and Nancy raced to her side.

"Lawsey, Miss Lady, I don't even know your name. Are you that German woman what lives in that little house down there by Grand River bridge?"

"I am. My name is Sarah. Sarah Yoder." Then Sarah's strong fingers straightened the heavy, tilting sack, while Marianne's gnarled, black hands scooped up the golden wheat.

"Oh lawsey, I do thank you. Missy Pearl done gonna be awful mad at me spillin' her last sack of wheat on the ground.

"Oh Lawd!" she proclaimed loudly. "Ain't these here hard times? trouble times, trouble times."

Indeed, these were "trouble times." Her mistress, Miss Pearl, was elderly and bedfast. Before she'd said farewell to her Confederate colonel husband, Buford Mansfred, she'd stripped her mansion of every silver piece. She'd collected all her gold, even twisting the rings from her swollen fingers.

Selling it all, she'd support the Confederate cause until they laid her in her grave. Yes, she would die a true Southern gentlewoman. All her fine horses had been given too, along with her milk cows and all her farm animals that could be sold for munitions, or butchered to feed the hungry, roving soldiers. Only one milk cow remained—old Molly.

Sarah knew too that all her possessions were exposed to the dreaded jayhawkers from Kansas as well as the needy Confederate soldiers.

"Your man gone off to war?" Marianne's red-streaked eyes focused upon Sarah's face.

"Yes." She'd be truthful. She sensed that she could trust this slave woman whose whole life had been a life of sorrow.

"Why are you, a Northern woman, pickin' up this grain for this old slave woman? Ain't we on different sides?"

Outwardly, there were factions and sides. But Sarah had been taught that God is impartial and causes the sun to shine on everyone. Christ called us to love, not hate. "There is neither Jew nor Greek, male nor female, slave nor free...."

"My husband's in the Union forces." Sarah's tongue attempted to get used to saying those words. They jarred and twisted her heart each time her tongue brought them forward.

Then Marianne, who'd thrust the one hundred pound sack on her shoulder, turned toward the mill and cried out: "Oh hallelujah! The day of redemption is near. Pres'dent Lincoln, he's gonna free this old slave woman."

So Sarah and Nancy had befriended the old black woman. She knew that Miss Pearl and her last remaining slave woman were facing the same dreadful hardship and oncoming winter that she and Nancy and old Mack Sherman faced.

"Have you lived here in Missouri all your life?" Sarah inquired.

"Lawsey, no, Miss Sarah, lawsey no. Born down in Mississip. Forty years in the cotton fields. Massa seen I'm too old for field work, so's he put me in the kitchen. Then he sold me up river. Massa Mansfred, he done bought this old bag o' bones. I cooks for Miss Pearl these last ten years."

At the look of almost overwhelming sorrow in Marianne's eyes, Sarah felt a heaviness and the pain of the old woman's suffering.

"Northern lady gonna suffer too. This war is like the wind tore loose. It burns everywhere and don't know nothing 'bout North and South."

Then old Marianne shifted and lowered her sack and focused her eyes upon Sarah's belly. "You gonna have a hard time, child comin' this here winter and no man to split wood and do for you."

Sarah was now four months along and was beginning to show. She'd been too occupied with the portions that life had shoved in front of her lately to take much thought for herself. Guess she'd have to tell Nancy soon. Well, she did have old Mack Sherman, he would help do for them.

"Lawsey, Miss Sarah." Marianne's face broke into a blissful smile, showing her red tongue and broken teeth. "Lawsey, ain't God merciful? You comin' due 'bout February, an' me nearby on that hill yonder.

"You send your hired man and old Marianne'll come. Why, I was the birthin' woman for all the women on Massa's plantation down there in Mississip. Yes, old Marianne'll help do for you when that child starts pushin'. I's seen more baby bottoms, black or white, than any woman this side of the Mississip River."

Chapter 7

Old Prince, blind in one eye, spavined and sway-backed, made feeble attempts to pull the wagon down the cornrow. Sarah and old Mack grabbed the corn ears, shucked them, then tossed them against the high buckboard of the wagon.

The ten acres of corn had produced bountifully, but they needed to get it harvested before the rains came and the horse and the wagon mired in the bottomless mud.

Sarah's corn ears hit the buckboard with a loud bang. She was angry. She worked out her anger right there through stripping those corn stalks of their fat ears, then tossing them with a speed that shamed old Mack.

Bushwhackers! Bushwhackers! Yes, the ragamuffin bushwhackers from Bates County had ridden through two nights ago, relieving them of their milk cows. Tillie, Bossy, and Brindle, with fear-glazed eyes, tails high in the air, staggered and bellowed down the road toward Batestown.

"Oh God," she prayed, without breaking the rhythm of her corn husking. "No cows, no milk, no cheese or butter, and winter coming and this new child growing in my belly."

If she could only hear from Solomon. Was he warm enough on these cold autumn nights? Did he meet others of his faith who were so torn in spirit? Did he have to carry a gun? They called those Sharps rifles the soldiers carried "Beecher's

Bibles," after Henry Ward Beecher, that New York preacher who helped raise funds for the killing instruments. Sarah couldn't allow herself to even think of Solomon firing a gun.

Yes, Solomon carried a "Beecher's Bible." But did he, like his brethren back in Virginia, fire it at the treetops and not at the advancing soldiers? It had been reported that a number of Mennonites and Dunkers had caused General Stonewall Jackson to say:

> There lives a people in the Valley of Virginia, that are not hard to bring to the army. While there they are obedient to their officers. Nor is it difficult to have them take aim, but it is impossible to get them to take correct aim. I, therefore, think it better to leave them at their homes that they may produce supplies for the army.

It was reported that John A. Showalter was severely persecuted and endured a court-martial for refusing to drill, and was finally permitted to serve as army cook.

Sarah kept hoping for news. Had he been caught in the bloody battle at Lone Jack, twenty miles away, or wounded in the fierce battle at Lexington on the Missouri River?

> Because thou hast made the Lord, which is my refuge, even the most high, thy habitation; there shall no evil befall thee, neither shall any plague come nigh thy dwelling, for he shall give his angels charge over thee, to keep thee in all thy ways.

The words soothed her troubled soul. She grabbed another ear of corn, hanging heavily down toward the rich earth. Toil, backache, and weariness—day after day—it kept her mind occupied. She felt the presence of God when she worked. When she worked, she did not worry and despair.

The worries, though, were waiting to surface. How

would she pay Mack, her hired man? Would their supply of wood last through the icy blasts of winter? What about Nancy? Sarah could only pray that Nancy, who'd taken over most of the cooking lately, would gain courage from the way she herself lived through such troublesome times. Thank God the child within her womb was growing strong—she could feel the kicks against her belly now. She was a strong woman. When her time came, surely God with his mercy above and nature here below would assist her.

Then she chuckled. Even when the winds of war are blowing over one's head, one could still laugh. That day she and Nancy met old Marianne at the mill she had noticed a hand-painted sign posted in the Commercial Hotel window. "Baker needed—inquire within." Well, if anyone needed cash in her pocket, it was Sarah Yoder.

Nancy'd held the reins while she went in. Sarah was eager for some real hard cash (wouldn't silver be wonderful?), for she was down now to only thirty-seven cents. That was it.

"Yes, I need someone to bake bread for these endless troops an' God only knows who that keep passing through here every day," Stoner Hite, the hotel manager, had told her.

So she had taken Nancy and the flour back to the safety of the house with old Mack nearby. She had saddled up Old Prince to ride back to the hotel where she'd show them how to bake the best bread any of them ever sank their teeth into. Pshaw! For Sarah Yoder, baking bread was easy as humming and singing .

CHAPTER 8

It took Sarah a few minutes to get her bearings in the oversized kitchen. Once she'd organized her bowl, flour sifter, found the rolling pin, and checked the huge cast-iron oven, she rolled up her calico sleeves to commence.

Kneading bread is just the thing for working out the soreness of one's heart and soul. She threw in the yeast, tossed in a measure of flour, then hurried over to the cast-iron stove for the heavy, black teakettle and poured in a goodly amount of the scalding water. Next, Sarah mixed and stirred, wiping the sweat off her cheeks with a raised shoulder. Whew! It was a scorcher of a day.

Well, she'd been a bit uncertain about it, being out of her own kitchen, and mixing this awful batch of dough. No, she hadn't baked so much bread since helping her mother get ready for the meeting at their house on Sunday, back in Ohio. But, the way she was getting into it, she'd have the twenty golden-crusted loaves, brushed with butter, done in time to get back and help Nancy with the evening chores. Money in her pocket to boot! Then she hummed and sang, heartened by the thoughts of real silver coins in her pocket.

Kneading the huge batch of dough, she divided it out into the pans to rise. Stoking up the fire, sweat running down her back, she sat down to rest her tired feet.

But, something was wrong. Sarah's dough just sat there.

It wasn't rising. She walked over to look at it, savoring the aroma. Her mind raced back over the steps she'd taken. What was the matter?

Well, she'd wait a little longer. Then realizing that the supper hour would come and Mr. Stoner Hite would demand real loaves to feed his hungry evening hordes, she grew desperate. She realized finally that the scalding water had killed the yeast, and that her dough—white, flour-covered, savory—could sit there until the geese flew south for the winter, but that it would never rise.

Never had any woman worked faster than Sarah, trying to beat the clock for the evening rush. Sift, sift, roll, roll, pound and knead. Knead, pound, divide, knead again. Sweat broke through her dress in the back. Her long legs braced her body; her feet lifted and shifted to support the movements of her waist and arms.

Her body ached. Wisps dislodged from her hair. The clock struck three-thirty. "God help me," she prayed. She looked ashamedly over in the corner to the broken old apple basket where she'd dumped the sorry, uncooperative dough. She'd get rid of it later. She'd never have Mr. Hite, or any other person, for that matter, say that Sarah Yoder was a failure at baking bread.

Flour smudged her face. She'd done it. Baked twenty-three loaves, all golden browned and full risen and round topped. Her mouth watered at the aroma of the fresh baked loaves.

Mr. Hite had come back to the kitchen wondering when she'd be finished. He'd paid her two silver dollars and had given her a loaf of bread to take home to boot. He allowed as, yes, he'd be pleased if she could come back tomorrow and help him out. But Sarah never came back, and never after that tried her hand at baking bread for hotel folks.

Ashamed of the waste and the humiliating mistake, she'd covered the basket of miserable fallen dough with her sunbonnet, unbuttoned and stretched over it. She tucked the basket, heavy with the disgraceful dough, close to her side. Her brow would just have to bear the heat of the sun. Maybe, she hoped, the full basket at her side would pass for a basket of laundry if anyone who knew her passed her on the street.

Then, leading Old Prince, she knew just what she'd do. She couldn't leave the sinful remnants of her failure behind. But it was the worst mistake she ever made in her life, much worse than scalding the yeast.

Sarah'd wait until she got down there by the grist mill and the mill trace. The shameful fallen dough would find its hiding place at the bottom of Mill Creek. Yes, it would sink, heavy as lead. Food for the catfish. Turning, she saw a few uniformed Union soldiers heading up the hill. A farmer in his wagon lumbered toward her, cracking his whip over the backs of his black-coated team. No one seemed to be watching her.

There by the stand of willows, just north of the mill, she let Old Prince eat some sour dock while, with both arms, she lifted the shameful basket over the rail fence, and heaved the fallen dough into the deepest water which flowed downward toward the mill.

Nobody ever needed to know about Sarah Yoder's bread dough failure up at that hotel. The silver coins clinked in her pocket as she mounted Old Prince, heading him on down the dirt road toward the mill, then on towards Grand River and her farm.

Old Prince sneezed, looked back at her with glazed eyes, then stumbled. What was that up ahead? A motley crowd had suddenly gathered at the edge of Brodie's mill by the big cottonwood trees. She could hear jeering, laughing, and hooting sounds. Then she noticed arms extended with fingers pointed right towards the giant moss-covered mill wheel, faithfully splashing, turning, splashing.

Hoots of laughter drifted toward her. Then before God above and the jeering crowd, right before her bewildered eyes she saw the reason for such belly-shaking laughter. There, climbing up the paddle of the mill wheel rose her shameful dough. It hadn't been heavy enough to sink to the bottom.

The sorry dough plopped and stretched like taffy, while the crowd jeered and hooted. Sarah ducked her head in shame, kicking Old Prince with her heel in a futile attempt to break him into a gallop and pass the scene which revealed her folly. Face red with shame, her ears burned at their cries:

"Well now, old Brodie here at this mill not only grinds the wheat into flour, he even uses his mill wheel to knead the dough. Everybody come back in the mornin', reckon he'll have some loaves baked fresh fer us!"

If you had looked westward toward those rising trees by Grand River, you would have seen a tall woman leaning over the head of her horse, hightailing it for home, fast as Ichabod Crane's race through the dark woods of Sleepy Hollow.

Chapter 9

That fall Special Order Number Twelve was issued from Major Thomas Bigger's desk at Fort Harrisonville. This order commanded Captain Tillotson and a small band of Union soldiers to scour the country around Grand River for guerrillas and bushwhackers, to use diligence and to return to camp by evening.

But as with all wars, great evil jars loose and the innocent are caught in its jaws. The soldiers did not use diligence. Unable to find the band of cutthroat bushwhackers, they'd ransacked farm homes of Southerners or those of suspected rebel sympathy.

Most Southerners and rebel sympathizers had already fled south and eastward. At sunset, the band of fifteen Union soldiers, fortified by the wine found in abandoned basements and cellars, exploded with animated revelry in their decision to light up the evening sky by setting fire to that old Confederate Colonel's brick mansion high on that windswept hill.

Miss Pearl died that evening—died from a stroke and the smoke and flames of the burning. Her weary body and anguished mind could no longer bear the pain and loss of a time and era that was vanishing before her.

When Marianne, who'd been out in the farthest pasture searching for their only remaining cow, looked back, she froze in fear at the flames leaping from the mansion roof, dancing in the western sky. She knew she would not be able to get there in time to help her Miss Pearl.

Then a great weight of sorrow overcame Marianne. The weariness of her sixty-three years of living, burdened as a slave, swept over her spirit. The ragged edges of the pain of having three children torn from her bosom to be sold "down river," the scars of her beatings when her cotton sack had not weighed enough—all this and much more rose up, and her soul bled as the huge house and Miss Pearl went up in the red flames.

"Oh, merciful Jesus." She wept, kneeling in the ditch where she hid, holding the rope tied to Molly, the cow.

"Oh, merciful Jesus, what's gonna happen to this old slave woman?"

Her eyes rolled in fear for her life. She knew that roving bands of guerrillas and drunken soldiers were not above shooting "niggers" for fun and sport. This, after all, was a land without law.

She implored God above in mercy to guide her now. God did guide Marianne. He was nearer than the tears streaming down her cheeks or the shiny scars on her back. For did not Jesus, the Son of God, also bear such scars, and did not he die as a slave?

Marianne rolled and rocked in the ditch, grasping the rope that held Molly as she emptied her spirit with the songs of slaves: "Dark midnight was my cry, give me Jesus. Dark midnight was my cry, give me Jesus."

Down beyond the tall oaks and cottonwoods by the river, Sarah grabbed a soiled envelope, clasping it to her heart as she raced toward the kitchen. Mack Sherman had plodded into town to the post office, making the weekly journey on the swayback Old Prince. Since he still had two jugs of apple jack in the barn, he spent a few cents for a twist of tobacco.

Nancy, folding the wash she'd just removed from the clothesline behind the porch, dropped a dish towel and raced to her mother.

"A letter from Father?"

"Yes, thank God. News from Father." Sarah tore open the envelope with a chapped finger. Her eyes burnt holes in the torn sheet with a few lines scribbled in lead pencil upon it.

"Dearest Family. I pray each day that God above will stop this war. I cannot tell you much about it, only that I am safe. I do not understand what men are doing to each other in this country. I pray each hour that you and Nancy are well. Remember to read the holy Scriptures and from *Martyrs Mirror*."

Then, near the bottom she read: "The captain said that he was tired of watching me shoot the leaves in the tops of the trees, so they moved me to kitchen duty. Sometimes, I help with the wounded.

"I pray that the war will end soon. Tell Nancy to study her arithmetic and her reader too. Your affectionate husband, Solomon Yoder."

So Solomon Yoder found at least a partial solution to the awful pangs of his conscience. Sarah, tears of thankfulness to God streaming down her cheeks, folded the torn paper, and slipped it inside the bosom of her dress, where she could take it out through the day, letting the words comfort her soul.

Chapter 10

The next morning frost lay in thick layers upon the fence rails, fallen leaves, and corn stalks. Here and there smoke rose up from assorted chimneys across the land.

With winter coming, Sarah and Mack Sherman concentrated on cutting, dragging, and stacking together as much wood for the fireplace and kitchen stove as they could.

They'd decided to separate it into three piles: a small one behind the house, a larger one inside an empty corner of the barn, covered with wheat straw to keep it hidden, and another one, cut but unsplit, just inside the edge of the woods. If bushwhackers came to plunder and steal, maybe this way the hidden wood would spare them from the winter's freezing blasts.

Sarah walked heavily now. She'd been eating well, with all the fall garden they'd stored, plus her canning. Still, both she and Nancy needed milk. It worried her, with this child coming. She thought of her potatoes lining the shallow bin near the floor of their small root cellar. All such stored food comforted her.

The only thing was, they might be short of meat. She and Mack talked of butchering Barney, the spotted pig, but she'd prefer to wait until he gained more weight. On the other hand, Barney was in daily danger of being stolen, same as her cows. That made her feel sad and angry. So many decisions.

The child within her belly kicked hard with healthy regularity. Wasn't it a blessing, God sending her and Solomon another child after almost eleven years? But was it really? These troubled times, with war descending upon them?

Nancy, when she finally told her the news, hugged her with joy. Such a child, so angel like. If only Nancy would protest once in awhile. The child, growing but still thin, only smiled and seemed to ask for more work to do.

There was something she didn't tell Nancy, though. She didn't tell her how much she would be comforted by a visit from a Mennonite or even a Dunker woman from over east beyond the hill.

All worship services and gatherings among these Anabaptists had been halted. They were so few and scattered. She'd heard that the Sherman Hartzlers—all of them—had hidden out in the woods, way over by Camp Branch, fearing for their very lives as rebel bushwhackers had raided their region, burning haystacks, barns, plundering houses. "Oh," thought Sarah, "if only when my time comes, I wouldn't be alone."

She knew that if she let herself stop the weary chores and endless tasks needed for their survival her faith might falter and the fear would mount. Her thoughts were her prayers: "He shall cover thee with his feathers, and under his wings shalt thou trust; his truth shall be thy shield and buckler."

Oh yes. Solomon had put down his gun. "May God's truth also be Solomon's shield in these stormy, heartbreaking days of war," she breathed.

Then Sarah walked out on the porch to shake out the braided hearth rug. She was startled by two staggering figures lumbering down the slope, partially hidden by the trees in the bend.

Her dark eyes strained to see. Two black objects came into focus, both with rolling, heavy gait. Why if it wasn't that old slave woman, Marianne. What was she leading behind her? A cow?

It was Marianne. A stick over her shoulder held a ragged pack bound in cloth, while her other hand, bare to the cold, drug the black milk cow, Molly. Dropping her rug, Sarah quickened her pace to the gate.

"Lawsey, Miss Sarah. Is that you? O thank the Lawd for done savin' me!"

"Marianne!" Sarah started running, her extended belly swinging. Before she could ask, "What happened?" a flood of tears rolled toward her.

"Miss Sarah, this old black slave woman ain't got no home no more." She dropped her rope while the tired Molly mooed, stretching out her tongue for a branch of frost-laced asters by the roadside.

"The devil done sent his soldiers. They drunk and do nothin' but howl and plunder."

Sarah guided Marianne through the gate, which was wide enough for poor old Molly, too.

"Come with me. Sit with us in the kitchen while I get you something hot to eat and drink." It was apparent that tragedy had struck.

Homeless Marianne let herself be led like a little child. She sat in the split willow rocker by the fireplace, holding her knapsack, tears still streaming.

Then Sarah heard the shocking tale of pillage and burning. How Marianne herself had picked up the charred body of Miss Pearl and buried her at the soft edge of the garden.

Marianne had been too overcome with fright to venture into town alone to get the Episcopalian priest to perform a funeral service. She crumbled, like a child cowering in a corner, her resources exhausted.

Marianne began to take heart by the warm presence of Nancy and Sarah, and by the comfort of the blazing fire.

"Would you like another cup of tea?" asked Nancy, patting her shoulder, tears in her eyes over the plight of the sad old Marianne.

"Lawsey child, but this old black woman eatin' your corn pone, drinkin' your tea, an' your own Pa done gone off to fight the war. Lawd save us!"

Marianne did hold out her tin cup while Sarah handed her a thick chunk of cornbread.

And so the winds of the border wars blew over that verdant land, bringing together, mercifully, an old slave woman, an Amish Mennonite woman, great with child, and her innocent fairskinned daughter, Nancy.

Together, God breathing grace and strength upon them, they would find a way through until the smoke and din of war was lifted. And, do not forget old Mack Sherman, out in the shed searching for his jug of apple jack. Isn't he one of God's creatures, too? Did not God also send poor old Mack Sherman? Yes, they were four, facing the thickening gloom of war together.

Sarah's eyes searched the fading Fraktur brought from Pennsylvania by her people to Ohio, and now here on her wall by the fireplace. The words comforted her:

> If thou but suffer God to guide thee
> And hope in Him through all thy ways,
> He'll give thee strength, what 'ere betide thee,
> And bear thee through the evil days.
> Who trusts in God's unchanging love
> Builds on a rock that naught can move.

Then too, don't forget. God also sent them a cow. More mercy.

Putting down her empty tin cup, Marianne rocked in the chair and shouted loudly, "Am I free now? Am I a free woman now? Please God, am I free?"

According to the law, Marianne was not a free woman yet. It was not until January 1, 1863, that President Lincoln issued the final order as the Emancipation Proclamation, but even that did not free slaves in the border states.

Chapter 11

By December they'd settled into the routine of their new living arrangement. However, Sarah'd learned that in times of war, nothing was routine.

They took Nancy's small wooden bed down, moving it out by the fireplace for Marianne. Nancy would sleep with Sarah.

They'd spread Marianne's bed with the yellow and brown patchwork quilt given to them by Grandma Rebecca Yoder, back in Ohio. Marianne allowed as to how there was only one place in the small farmhouse for her: "Right here by the fire. Old Marianne never lets the fire go out. Besides, the coals warm these old bones. Put old Marianne here by the fire." Then she chuckled, "I watch the fire and keep the evil out."

Comforted by the warm presence of Marianne, Sarah awaited her time. Nancy, joyfully anticipating the arrival of a baby, rose to the occasion. A quick learner, she now baked the fresh bread each week. She hadn't mastered soda biscuits yet, but Marianne had promised to teach her.

Nancy still looked thin, especially with her golden hair braided and wound around her pale face with its delicate features. Sarah sometimes looked at her and couldn't help thinking, Why is she so frail looking? And here they were, called upon to live in these rugged exhausting times.

Even with Solomon's absence, they could feel more secure now, like a family. Marianne assured Sarah daily, "I'm the best birthin' woman this side of the Mississip!"

Sarah believed her, too. She'd taken heart by Marianne's doctoring skills. Last month, Nancy, caught in a cold November rain while coming from the barn where she'd been milking Molly, came down with a dreadful hacking cough.

Sarah hadn't been able to rest at all with the awful cough and the fever that heated Nancy's face.

Then they'd heard heavy footsteps and floorboards squeaking. This was followed by the clang of the iron poker against the hearth and crane, as Marianne stoked up the fireplace, putting the iron teakettle on to boil.

Next, Marianne had rummaged through that faded knapsack she'd brought from the blazing walls of Miss Pearl's mansion.

Shoving open the bedroom door, she had stood there, face shining, eyes wide. Her billowing flannel nightdress cascaded to the floor. "Lawsey, old Marianne's got the medicine for the cough."

Yes, Marianne was not only a renowned midwife, but a respected healer with her herbs and potions.

Bracing up the fevered child, her thick fingers thrust the tin cup near Nancy's lips.

"Honey and fennel seed tea. I boiled it for the cough. Drink all this here fennel tea. Old Marianne ain't gonna allow Miss Nancy to die of pneumonie."

Strangely enough, the fennel tea brought relief. Nancy's cough subsided and she drifted off into a blissful sleep.

When the birth pangs started in her swollen belly, Sarah might not have a Mennonite or Dunker woman from over the hill with her, but the strength and presence of Marianne brought comfort. It was from God above, this trust that dwelt among them. And the cow, Molly, was a blessed miracle sent from heaven.

Old Mack Sherman, though, had thrown a fit. "Ain't gonna have no nigger woman in my house," he'd complained.

But Mack had Nancy's small room to himself come nights and the barn by day.

Besides, didn't he comfort himself considerably with his jugs of apple jack anyway? Old Mack's protests and prejudices eased. Deep within, he even took comfort at the presence of that old black woman who looked as if she was filled with the wisdom of the ages.

Actually, Mack was afraid of her. He knew that in Sarah's hour of need, Marianne had strong hands to give support, and on this point, Mack Sherman was surely relieved. He'd once helped a Cheyenne Indian woman give birth, way out in Kansas Territory. No more of that for him.

Then, came butchering day. Nancy still chuckled about the butchering day. Now with cold weather and Barney the pig all fattened up, they had decided that maybe they'd better get the butchering over with before those roving bushwhackers stole him.

"Yes, pshaw, I ain't no dummy," pleaded old Mack, wiping his nose on the cuff of his frayed coat.

"Yes, I know how to butcher a hog," he'd told Sarah with a petulant whine.

Near full-term and heavy as she was, Sarah knew she'd need plenty of help. She was strong, and in spite of her heaviness, could still step quickly. They, all four, would work together.

Marianne had spent a full hour sharpening the butcher knives on a broken piece of grindstone. "Ain't no butcherin' goin' on here 'till I've got my knives sharp. Cain't stick no hog with a dull knife."

On that cold brisk day, thank God, the sun shone with splendor and brilliance. Mack, leaning in the wind, drug the logs together beneath the great cast-iron kettle. "Cain't butcher without lots of boilin' water," allowed Mack.

But what was really worrying Mack was pulling the trigger on that ancient rifle and shooting Barney. Then too, could he leap up with one of those knives sharpened like razors by that old slave woman and cut Barney's throat? He started to worry some more.

Well, guess once he'd get this fire good and started beneath this kettle, he'd go back to the barn to settle down his nerves some, at least, with a generous cupful or two of the apple jack he'd saved over from two years ago.

Yes, nerve medicine like that was certainly meant for a special day like this when all his skills and talents were needed.

Sarah put on a heavy, warm coat and tied a woolen scarf over her head. She'd cleared the back porch and made a table out of boards and saw horses. There in the cold they'd have space to cut the fresh meat. They'd pool their strength. By tomorrow they could sink their teeth into fresh sausage and fried mush. Already her mouth watered.

Nancy, dressed as warmly as her mother, pitied poor Barney, but tried not to dwell on it. She was old enough now that she'd learned full well that life around here was, at least, a life of sacrifice.

Now it was Barney's turn. "Yes," Nancy'd allowed. "I'll help Marianne strip and clean hog entrails." But, since she'd never before done it, she really didn't know what she was saying.

Water boiled and bubbled in the kettle. The rope and pulley, slung over the maple tree limb, was ready for old Barney's carcass. They'd lower his fat sides and buttocks down into a barrel of scalding water to loosen his bristles. Then they'd all begin scraping his hide with Marianne's razor-edged knives.

"I'm gonna make the cracklins. I'm the plantation cracklin woman." Marianne smiled broadly and chuckled. This was a high day for her.

"Then when it's all over, I makes the soap."

All agreed that it was time to begin. And, to begin butchering means to take the first awful step.

Mack, fortified by two whole cupfuls of his apple jack, took down the worn rifle and wobbled out to the pigpen. His dirty pants billowed in the cold wind.

"Ah," thought Mack, "Why there ain't nothin' to this here butcherin.'"

Bumping against the rails of Barney's pigpen, Mack blinked, trying to clear his eyes.

"Blast it," he mumbled. For Mack, warmed by his blessed apple jack, saw two fat hogs. "Why cain't that there Barney stand still?"

Behind, about forty yards, waddled Marianne, sides heaving, wrapped in a woolen sweater. Her face glistened, black and solid as the Sphinx. She ambled to the wood pile and grasped the sledge hammer in her thick hands.

Sarah and Nancy looked on nervously from the yard fence, there by the boiling kettle and hanging pulley. Anticipation filled the air. These four people had never walked this way before; but their trust was in God on this butchering day.

Old Mack aimed down the rusty gun barrel with his bleary eye. His dirty finger squeezed the trigger. There was an awful blast, jarring Mack, whose curse words mingled with poor Barney's piercing squeals.

"Oh, mother. Is he dead?" cried Nancy, both hands rising to her mouth. "Is Barney dead?"

Old Mack had aimed at one of the two pigs he'd seen, and he'd hit one of them at least. He grinned, wiped his drooling mouth with the back of his hand, and looked back over his shoulder towards Sarah and Nancy with a sick smile. Barney's screams rose up to heaven as he kept circling the pigpen.

"Get out of my way!" Mack was shoved, briskly, crudely, to one side. Marianne had sized up the situation and now with regal strength, she bore forward and took command.

"Get out of my way!"

Her arms raised the rusty sledgehammer above her head. She leaned into the pigpen.

Poor Barney, who'd only been slightly wounded in his ear, made his third shrieking circle around his pen. He was brought to a dead halt and his feet splayed beneath him by the force of Marianne's sledgehammer coming down right between his eyes.

"Give me that knife!" cried Marianne to the glazed-eyed Mack, who staggered backwards at her bulk and fearful strength.

"Cain't trust no poor white trash of a man come butcherin' time." She grumbled, her own prejudices leaking through.

Then she sliced open poor Barney's throat and the crimson blood burst out around Marianne's feet. "Ain't no time for no pussy-footed man. This here's butcherin' day."

From that time on, poor old Mack had to take the back seat. Marianne had established herself on that butchering day—established herself as capable and in command.

For, does not the Scripture say: "Every valley shall be exalted and every mountain and hill shall be made low; and the crooked shall be made straight, and the rough places plain."

"Bring that sled 'round here," she'd commanded. Mack, with a pitiful dip of his head, led Old Prince with the sled made of boards and two-by-fours around by the pigpen.

All four of them rolled poor Barney's carcass onto the sled. Marianne, now taking full control, took hold of Prince's reins herself, clucking her tongue.

"Giddy up, now!"

They scalded Barney and scraped his hide, but, why hadn't somebody reminded Nancy of what hog guts actually smelled like?

Standing on a block of wood before Barney's bulging belly hanging from that tree limb, Marianne aimed and stabbed with her razor-sharp knife. In just one fell swoop great billows of stinking hog guts rolled out into the tub beneath.

The warm guts, meeting the cold winter air, released their offal smells in the steam that rose above and clouded around their heads.

As time wore on, Mack became a little more steady. Subdued, he followed Sarah's directions as they chopped and cut up Barney's carcass. They laid out the portions to be smoked: hams, shoulders, side meat for bacon. Next, they laid aside the back bones, head meat, liver, and scraps for sausage.

Over on the back porch, Marianne and Nancy sat in those old bentwood chairs, partially hidden by the steam rising up around them.

All four of them carried buckets of water from the well, emptying them in a second wooden barrel. "Heave in the salt," hollered Marianne. It would take salt enough to float an egg. That's right. Nancy kept putting the egg in the cloudy water until she no longer needed her hand beneath it to keep it from sinking.

"Hams, then shoulders and bacon gonna soak here for two weeks. Yep. Then we's takin' them to the smokehouse. Mack Sherman, you'se gonna get the hickory chips."

Well, Mack, quite put out by having taken a lower rung on the ladder that day, raked his boot around the edge of the fire under the kettle, trying to put it out. He kept his thoughts to himself. He was burning inside. Why, didn't he know how to smoke meat without that old woman giving him directions?

The sun made its circle around to the west where it hid in a purple evening cloud. Nancy, tired, but chuckling, reckoned that, given her druthers, next time she'd aim the rifle or do the scalding.

Turning those hog guts inside out to empty them, scalding them, and soaking them in salt water hadn't actually been all that much fun. But Marianne had taught her a lot on butchering day. Nancy had never stuffed sausage before. She tried to overlook the grease everywhere.

Neither could she ever remember so much grease in the kitchen as they fried down the pork. Tomorrow, according to Marianne's instructions, they'd pack this fried down pork into those stone crocks and cover them with hog lard. Yes, butchering day had been a challenge.

She couldn't wait to help Marianne make soap afterwards. If only Father were here, so she could tell him about all this fun.

Chapter 12

Solomon had been away in the Union army for almost six months. He wished that he was not a part of this war machine, even though he now peeled potatoes and threw hastily constructed meals together, often in the poorest of circumstances, to help keep the moving troops from starving.

Occasionally, he was sent out to the battlefields, smoke just clearing. Here the victorious chased the fleeing heels of the defeated to begin bringing in the wounded and picking up the dead.

Solomon saw clearly one truth. War was an evil which produced even more evil. Surely there was not a thinking person alive, who when exposed to such death, stench, plunder, and destruction, would not lay down his rifle and plead for people to settle their disputes through dialogue, compromise, and arbitration until they could live peacefully together.

He lay on his back in the temporary barrack. Cold winter wind swept through the cracks in the weathered boarding. Heavy fatigue overwhelmed him. He began to doze. Oh, the stories he could tell the folks at home. His heart ached to embrace Sarah; he longed to reach out to Nancy.

He'd tried not to worry over the only letter he'd received from Sarah. The news that she was expecting a child in January nearly flattened him.

Listen to the anguish which stupefies the mind. Hear the

almost silent murmur in their hearts, a murmur that most will not admit they hear, "He who wields the sword, perishes with the sword."

War is built on greed, on deceit, on baseness in the hearts of humans. Glamorized and dressed up, it is trotted out to the masses as a way to achieve honor and glory.

When Solomon helped scoop up the fragmented and bloated bodies from the battlefields, when he looked into the glazed eyes of eighteen- and nineteen-year-old boys whose dead faces masked horror frozen in time, he vowed never again would he be a part of anyone's army.

"Lord, bring me safely home, and not me alone, but these others too, broken, freezing, these fathers and sons around me, these who may not have heard of the Christ of the cross," he prayed.

Solomon thought of the cross, the place where the Son of Man stretched out to die, absorbing the evil of the world. There, on that hewn wood, the Son of God taught us to "pray for those who spitefully use you."

His mind caught on the games of war where often accident, deceit, chance, and fate all have their way. Look at what happened at Waverly, Missouri, on the banks of that river town, swarming with Union forces, yet overrun by Confederate forces in August 1861. Accident, deceit, and chance ruled the day.

Captain Joseph Shelby of the Confederate army rallied his one hundred cavalrymen to the edge of the great timber overlooking the river at Waverly. Stringing a hemp rope across the mighty waters, they anchored a few rafts to the line, then placed riflemen on the bobbing logs.

Next, Captain Shelby had his men cut down a giant cottonwood tree. Stripping it of all limbs, they carefully trimmed it. Black paint was speedily brushed over the huge extended cylinder.

Heaving and levering, they managed to balance it

through forked stakes. The mighty mock cannon leered through the brush clinging to the riverbank. It glowered threateningly over the waters and toward the bend, awaiting the heavy Union riverboat, Sunshine, which would soon wend its way around the river bend and on up the river to Fort Leavenworth. There it would be relieved of its 500 Sharps rifles, over one hundred army wagons, and over a thousand sacks of flour, all intended to support the Union forces.

As the mighty riverboat neared the bend, Captain Shelby had a pitifully small band of his men on horseback drag tree branches back and forth across a small, dry plain. Columns of dust arose. He hoped the riverboat crew would be thrown off by thinking several hundred troops raised the dust on the cliff above the river.

Another small band, cowering in the bushes beneath the mock cannon, began to fire at the oncoming vessel. Soldiers behind the tree-log cannon moved it menacingly toward the smoking stacks of the steamboat.

When the ship was directly across from St. Thomas Wharf at Waverly, Captain Shelby marched out to the end of the wharf calling: "I am Captain Shelby of the Confederate army of the Confederate States of America. My river cannon is trained upon you. Surrender at once, or I shall give the order to blast you out of the water."

For a moment, silence prevailed.

Suddenly, overcome by fear and terror of being blasted out of the water by the awful cannon tilted at them, the Sunshine's captain ran up a white flag and slowly steamed over to the wharf. A Confederate victory was wrought of chance, deceit, accident, and wily craftiness.

When Solomon returned to his little frontier farm with his beloved, he could share these stories, and teach that enduring truth lived by many of his forbears who died in prison and went to the stake, rather than to take up arms against their fellow human beings.

One thing was for certain. The bloated corpses, the maimed men, the scorched countryside, and burned towns pointed clearly to Solomon what ought not to be. Surely, in this way still, the grace of God comes to us.

Solomon drifted off into a fitful but much needed sleep. Soon the bugle calls of reveille would jar his shattered nerves and mind to full consciousness again. Who rests well near a battlefield?

Chapter 13

Back at the little farm, a bright fire blazed in the fireplace, casting a golden light across the hearth. The wind howled at the eaves; the skies lowered—heavy, grey, almost scraping the cold, windswept landscape.

Nancy sat in the willow rocker, having just finished stirring the batch of golden batter of cornmeal. Marianne scraped it out of the wooden mixing bowl into the Dutch oven. The boards creaked under her heavy tread as she settled the cast-iron oven into the coals at the edge of the fire.

Nancy reached for the *Martyrs Mirror,* that huge volume that was read and treasured by people of her church. It contained the stories and accounts of martyrdom, especially of the Anabaptists of her faith.

She remembered her father's instruction to study her arithmetic. She'd filled the entire back of a brown paper bag with sums. Now, while the cornbread baked, she'd read again the story of Anna and Mary, the names she'd given to two young martyrs.

The candlelight flickered, keeping rhythm with the orange flickering from the logs in the fireplace. Nancy drew her stockinged feet under her in her chair. Tears began to glisten on her cheeks as she read of the two fifteen-year-old Anabaptist girls of Bamberg, Germany, in 1550. These were the years of the "Defenseless Christians," these thousands who were beheaded, drowned, and burned at the stake by the state church in the name of the Holy.

As she read, she could see Anna and Mary, who received Christ and because of their faith in him were baptized as adults. She read of their imprisonment which came as a result of their faithful stand. In prison they were tortured severely.

Marianne, checking the cornbread in the coals at the edge of the fire, noticed the girl's glistening cheeks.

"Lawsey, child, why do you read such a book that makes you cry? Lawsey, ain't there enough to make a body cry without readin' such a book?"

Then she sat by Nancy, half hoping the child would begin reading to her. She loved the Lord Jesus. She herself understood persecution, beatings, and being a castoff. When Nancy shared the *Martyrs Mirror* stories with Marianne, they struck a chord in her aching heart.

She couldn't help her inquiry. "Child, what are you readin'?"

"Oh, Marianne, the authorities want Mary and Anna to give up their faith in Jesus. They threw them into a prison and beat them."

"Oh, child, this old body knows about beatings. Did they give in?"

"Oh no! They were true to their baptismal vow." She wiped her cheek with her shoulder.

"Oh, I remember the day of my baptism. Deacon Whipple of the Methodist—the colored Methodist—he went ahead with a fence rail to sweep out the water moccasins while these old bones an' black skin crawl in the water."

"Buried with him in baptism! Glory, glory hallelujah!" Marianne's face still reflected some of the joy of the hour of her spirit's cleansing.

Nancy didn't know if she could tell the rest.

"They were condemned to death," she read with a choking voice. "Their persecutors, to reproach them, placed wreaths of weeds and straw upon their heads."

"Lawsey," interjected the soul-shaken Marianne, equally caught up in the account. "They wore the crowns, like the crown of the Lawd Jesus."

"And they said one to another: 'Since the Lord Christ wore a crown of thorns for us, why should we not wear these crowns of straw in honor of him?'"

By now they were both wiping tears with their kerchiefs. Nancy knew in her heart that when the war was over and they could again meet—these Mennonites and Dunkers—that she would present herself for such holy cleansing.

She would go down into the water with joy, or if the minister poured the water upon her head, what matter? She knew that already Christ had called her. Only the clouds of war must cease, then her people would meet.

There were others too, Dirk Eicher and Anna Holsopple, maybe they too would receive the holy cleansing. She knew they too loved the Lord Christ.

She continued the account: "Thus, the two maidens armored themselves with patience, according to their captain, Jesus, remained faithful unto death, died steadfastly and obtained, through grace, the glorious crown with God in heaven. They were led to execution as recorded. He who wishes may read this account, published by Johannes Manlius."

She closed the heavy volume, laying it on the worn bench. Marianne, rising, grabbed the handle of the Dutch oven, heaved it from the coals, and carried it into the kitchen.

Nancy, seeing her exhausted mother placing the ironstone plates on the rough-hewn table, stepped to her side. "Mother, Marianne and I will do it. You know we like to cook."

Sarah reached out and brought the fair child to her side. "I know, child, it's good for me to move around some; I'll not overdo. See if Mack is in from milking Molly."

Chapter 14

It had taken a few days for Mack to get over his hurt feelings on butchering day. But he soon saw that having Marianne here meant a lighter load for him. And since he allowed that he was getting old, this surely was a good thing. So he nodded and made peace with Marianne and ate her cornmeal with chunks of liver and cracklings in it. He savored it, shoveled it down, and even asked for more.

They sat around the table as the darkness settled. Sarah, in Solomon's absence, took the spiritual lead in the household. She bowed her white-covered head and prayed: "Oh merciful God, we give thee thanks for thy gift of Christ to us, and for our daily bread of which we are about to partake." She could hardly say the words without a break in her voice, but she prayed for God to guide and keep Solomon from danger, to bless his soul and bring him to the family hearth soon.

The moment she said "amen," Mack grabbed his spoon, slurped the broth from the top of his soup while reaching across the table for a healthy chunk of the cornbread. Oh, to warm his sides with these vittles. Mack, too, was thankful.

Sarah ate sparingly. She could hardly sit in the hard, straight-backed chair with such weight pulling her abdomen.

"I need to stand and take some steps," she said, rising. As she strode over to look out the eastern window of the kitchen to survey the falling snow swirling in the cold north wind, the first cramp sliced down her side.

She did not cry out. Sarah would not put on any unnecessary scene. She tried to stifle the traces of fear, the heavy sadness of Solomon's absence, and her loneliness. Then the pain struck again. She headed for her bed.

Marianne, sensing the hour, was in tune with every movement, each feeling expressed, any subtle change. "Child, your mamma's time is come. Rid up the table while I go help."

"Mack Sherman," she said as she looked at the bewhiskered old man, who was ducking and swilling his soup. Great pity for him rose up in her heart. They were both slaves, only in different ways, and it seemed that Mack was more bound than she. "Mack Sherman, you're needed to bring in the water. Fill the kettle, stoke the fire. Ain't gonna have the fire go out on a birthin' night. No siree."

Fear glazed old Mack's eyes. A birthing night, and he was caught here in this tiny house with three women, and maybe soon a howling baby. Oh, how he wanted a draft from his jug. Would he be able to find his reserve in the dark, in this storm?

He shoved his chair back, heaved himself into his ragged coat and pulled his stocking cap down over his ears. Yes, he would not fail to carry out Marianne's commands. He'd learned to carry out her orders on butchering day. His ears burned at the thought of it.

But, everybody knew, didn't they, that on a birthin' day or night, one always started with kettles of hot water. He wasn't sure what for, exactly, but he intended to do his part.

Would they be sending him for a doctor? Where would one find a doctor on a night like this, with war spilling all around them? All the doctors were busy sawing off the legs and arms of the wounded and searing the stumps with hot irons. Yes, he surely did need fortification for what lay ahead.

Lying on her back in bed, Sarah gave her mind and her body to the moment at hand, and her faith and her hope to God and the hours ahead.

She remembered. Nancy's birth had been long, painful, and difficult, but wasn't it always like that with the first one? Tonight would be different.

But, that night was not different. While the heavy snows descended in great swirls, shooting pains, like red-hot irons ripped at her belly. She arched, she clenched her teeth and rolled her head back in her feather pillow.

In the kitchen, Nancy followed Marianne's instructions. "Keep the fire a goin' an' the kettles boilin'." Then she reminded Nancy, "Say them verses you done memorized."

So, while Nancy stoked the fire with the split sticks of wood, she recited the words of solace in her mind: "God is our refuge and strength, a very present help in trouble. Therefore we will not we fear, though the earth be removed, and though the mountains be carried into the midst of the sea...the Lord of hosts is with us; the God of Jacob is our refuge."

What worried Marianne, besides Sarah's frightful pains, was the raging storm outside. The last time she'd looked in on Sarah, she hurried out to the fireplace and dragged the bentwood chair by her bedside. Here she'd stay. Her faithful Christian friend, Sarah, would have all her skill and comfort.

She searched her brain. She had her herbs, her potions—the ones for relaxing the muscles, the ones to stop the flow of blood. She closed her eyes. All of Marianne was in prayer—her mind, her body, her spirit.

By nine o'clock, Sarah could not help screaming out, just once. She didn't want to do it. "Do not frighten Nancy," she'd told herself. But the awful pangs of the flesh tore through the resolve made by her spirit.

By now Sarah knew that her travail would be long. She closed her eyes and prayed while the pains subsided. She hoped to get through this without the help of a doctor.

They'd talked about it; old Doc Barnum was up there in that makeshift war hospital, young men screaming and dying all around him. No, she could not take bread from the hungry, water from the famished. It could be her Solomon lying there. She could endure it alone.

Before the morning came, there was more travail, more body-splitting anguish, much more. Sarah, no longer able to keep her pain to herself, began to let it out.

Marianne searched in her knapsack for her leather shoe tongue. Finding it, she doubled it and slid it between Sarah's teeth for her to bite upon. She'd mixed chamomile—her herb for relaxing the muscles—with water, and spooned it into Sarah's cracked lips.

But, it seemed that nothing gave. She'd even taken that old sheet needed in emergencies and torn it into strips, twisting them into long pull ropes and attaching them to the bed posts.

Sarah pulled down as she bit her doubled shoe leather. Drenched in sweat, she prayed.

Outside, the dark, blustery night howled on. They'd agreed that if it seemed likely that they would need emergency help, Mack's job would be to saddle up Old Prince and ride for the doctor.

Nancy, in the kitchen, prayed and stoked her fire. Tears slid down her cheeks when she heard her mother's cries. Finally, she shook Mack, sitting there, stocking cap in hand, eyes glazed. "Oh, go for the doctor. Marianne, shouldn't Mack ride for the doctor?"

So out he bumbled into the cold, fearful night. Old Prince hadn't wanted to leave the barn. With fitful and slow steps he headed up the road, his old glassy eyes stinging in the blinding snow.

"Giddyap!" hollered Mack, but his cry was lost in the howls of the winter wind. When they finally came to the wooden bridge, Old Prince balked. Let others cross this awful place. He knew better. Like Martin Luther, the old horse said to himself, "Here I stand."

Mack broke down then, as he'd been trying to clean up his language with such Christian women praying and reciting verses all around him. He let the screaming wind and Old Prince's lowered ears hear curse words he hadn't used since he'd left those Indians in that camp back in Oklahoma Territory.

Mack was reduced to getting down off Old Prince. Wading in the deep snow, he tried to lead him across the bridge. Still, the horse wouldn't budge. Mack could only solve the problem by turning Prince around, remounting him, and taking that long route westerly, then north over the hill, and down toward the street where the doctor lived. But Mack's troubles weren't over.

When he and Old Prince got as far as Red Indian Saloon, both were in need of some kind of fortification. He wrapped the reins loosely around the post while he ambled in with freezing feet and dripping nose. A little nip of bourbon would help out mightily, wouldn't it?

Back in the little farmhouse almost lost in the blackness of the swirling snow, Sarah writhed in agony. Nancy went into her mother's room to hold her hand for awhile. Marianne mixed up another potion. The clock struck twelve-thirty. Still no Mack and no doctor. God was their only hope.

Returning to the kitchen, Nancy allowed as how she would dare the freezing back porch, and she opened the door facing the barn to see if Mack had arrived.

Dismayed, she saw a tall, lumbering, snow-covered animal, with head hanging, slide into the barn door as it swung open in the winter wind. Old Prince. He had returned. Where on earth were Mack and the doctor?

By three o'clock, it was all they could do to keep Sarah from slipping into unconsciousness. What next? What do the helpless do in the hour of extremity?

Marianne remembered Bertha Tobin, the leading cotton chopping slave woman down there in Mississippi. She had forgotten. They'd had to roll Bertha to get her baby to jar loose. Praise the Lord, now it came to her.

Half conscious, beyond giving assent, Sarah allowed her swollen body to be lowered out onto the hard floor.

This was more than serious. "Now you listen here to old Marianne, child, we're gonna need to work together. You get on that side of your ma, roll 'er plum over this here way, and I'll roll her back. Jars the baby loose."

They rolled poor Sarah's pain-pierced and weary body back and forth on the hard pine floor. Each moment seemed an eternity.

At last, Sarah gave a great cry as her last hour of labor set in.

They got her back on her bed. "Git the hot cloths ready," Marianne commanded. Nancy vanished into the kitchen again.

Nancy heard the newborn's cry at four-thirty in the morning. She wanted to rush in, to hold her mother's precious head, to kiss her, and then look at the child. But Marianne commanded, "Not yet, you stay there in the kitchen. I gotta tie this string." Soon Marianne hollered, "Bring me them cloths, child, and come here and see this baby girl."

They did not immediately name the tiny newborn, who lay peacefully on a torn square of flannel in Marianne's huge hands. They'd do that later. There was more work to be done.

Nancy took down the twists of sheet ropes. Marianne placed the tiny infant into the clothes basket, covered it warmly, and then turned to bathe Sarah Yoder's hot, perspiring brow.

Sarah was lost in a deep sleep. Her travail seemed over. Marianne and Nancy emptied pans and rinsed out the hot cloths. Finally, together, they spread the patchwork quilt over Sarah's body, tucking it gently to keep out any draft.

"You can lie down on my bed now, child. Old Marianne'll sit here till mornin' comes. Thank the Lawd, He done got us through the night."

Sarah stirred and moaned. Her face paled. She seemed to sink. Marianne's nodding head rose to her duty. Heaving back the covers she saw crimson streaks soaking down into the bed.

Blood. "Merciful God!"

Marianne heaved like a stricken antelope. Her legs lifted her bulk as she leaped to the kitchen and to her knapsack. "A pan of water. A pan of water, child. Bring it fast!"

Running to the kitchen, Nancy poured water from the iron tea kettle. She grabbed some of the soft flannel cloths she'd been cutting into squares. Reaching the bedroom, she paled at the sight of her mother. Her face was ghostly white; her sheet was stained blood red. Fear clutched Nancy's heart.

Marianne dug in her knapsack. Great fatigue swept over her, yet this was a crisis hour. "Oh Lawd God above!" She prayed. She searched with her tired, streaked eyes for her packet of dried persimmon leaves. She couldn't find it.

"Marianne, Marianne!" Nancy's voice, filled with terror, swept into her ears. Still, Marianne's thick fingers searched. She emptied the knapsack inside out, but to no avail.

Where on earth was her dried persimmon potion? Then, desperately, she remembered. On butchering day, Mack had cut his thumb with one of her razor-sharp knives. She had soaked a bandage in persimmon leaf water and applied it to the nasty cut to stop the bleeding. It must be in the pocket of her heavy coat behind the door by her bed.

When the small package of powerful potion was in her hand at last, she ripped it open, threw the ragged leaves into a chipped basin, and drenched them with hot water. "Seep, seep, Lawdy, let it not be too old," she prayed.

She held the potion-soaked cloth firmly against Sarah's soft flesh. Then Marianne brought her great, heavy fist straight down on Sarah's lower abdomen, pressing hard against the womb.

The fatigue-ridden old woman, now an instrument of a strength beyond her own, gave herself—body and spirit—to saving this frontier woman. Marianne looked heavenward, way past the rude ceiling boards, into those spaces seen by the afflicted and suffering, such as slaves at the whipping post and dying men upon crosses.

All of her was prayer. Her lips mumbled ancient words, prayers her grandmother taught her in the language of Africa. Those who rely on science alone would sneer at her waters and her potions, let alone her prayers.

Nancy Yoder herself trembled at the awe-filling mystery of the strange words ascending out of the old slave woman's mouth. It was as if she herself was at the extreme of affliction, at the very edge of a precipice facing a bottomless chasm. She kept on pressing her cloth with her fist, and murmuring her entreaties. And is it not written: "Out of the depths I cry to thee, O Lord! Lord, hear my voice! Let thy ears be attentive to the voice of my supplications!"

Yes, these were simple, unsophisticated people, but faith does not rely on sophistication and high levels of learning. No, it is of a different dimension, flowing out of that very part of the soul that touches God.

When the bleeding stopped, Sarah Yoder's riddled body, bruised and packed with Marianne's potion soaked cloths, was shifted. Pillows were placed under her lower body, raising it.

Sarah's head lay low. White as the winter snow upon the ledge of the window, she lay, breathing slowly, sleeping. Sarah Yoder would live.

Chapter 15

They named the tiny infant Barbara. She smiled at them with her piercing, dark eyes. Ringlets of coal-black hair covered her head.

Aside from the cries emitted at her birthing, the infant scarcely made a noise. Sarah held the newborn close to her breast, kissing her soft curls. She gave thanks for her own improving health.

A week had gone by and Sarah had been up on her feet for two hours this morning. Faith, the grace of God, and Marianne's skillful hands had brought her through. She felt her strength returning. The words circled in her mind: "O give thanks to the Lord, for he is good; for his steadfast love endures for ever!" They had experienced it, this enduring love.

The agony and strain of the night of her tiny sister's birth, however, had taken its toll on Nancy. Fatigue swept over her.

They put her in Marianne's bed by the fireplace where she could look out of the window and be comforted by the cheering fire against the bitterness of the cold outside. Sarah was worried. Why did the child look so pale? She noticed that Nancy hadn't finished all of the broth with potatoes that Marianne had fixed for her.

"I'm too tired now, Marianne. Later." She'd touched the blessed old calloused hand and held it for a moment. A wisp of a smile spread over her red lips as she drifted into a deep sleep.

Then, a body-shaking cough developed. Not a cold, nor the flu, nor the fever and ague, but a deep, hacking cough that left her drenched in sweat and even weaker.

Then she rallied. Nancy took more of Marianne's rich broths and soups. She gained enough strength to help her mother—especially to cradle the baby, Barbara, and sing her a cooing song. How she loved the bright-eyed baby.

Finding the strength, she asked Marianne if she could make the cornbread for supper. It felt good, stirring the golden meal again. But, when it was finished and baking on the hearth, her arm was weary. She wanted to lie down. Deep sleep followed.

Oh yes. Mack had come home—sheepish, head bowed, uncombed, ashamed. Overcome by the bourbon he'd gulped down that awful night at the Red Indian Saloon, it'd taken him a day and a half to revive. He'd slept through the blasting storm in a small room in the back of the saloon, along with a couple of Indian comrades who refused to go outside in the cold.

A part of Mack was so ashamed, so afraid, to come home. What were his choices? He was old, almost penniless, and had failed miserably in his duties. War and pestilence were all around. He would brave any rebukes dished out by that old slave woman. He could stand that, he guessed. But to be harangued by Sarah Yoder or by Nancy, that would be hard medicine to take.

Sarah, caught back from the cliffs of death, and Nancy, who seemed only made of kindness, forgiveness, and pity, were in no mood for castigating Mack.

After all, he'd tried. The poor horse, the war, the ghastly winter night had all congealed against him. They pitied him.

Nancy ran forward and took his grimy, cold hand. "Oh, Mack Sherman, you're back. I worried that you'd frozen to death. I'm so glad." She clutched at the shaggy arm of his coat. "Sit down. Oh, Marianne, make him some hot porridge. Mother, thank God, Mack's back home."

When Mack Sherman saw the tears in the fair child's eyes, his eyes, too, clouded over with tears. He honked his nose in a dirty rag, dropping heavily into the bentwood chair. Yes, he was ready for some home cooked victuals, that was for sure.

Sarah walked over to his chair and bent over to look into his eyes with kindness. "You tried, and I thank you with all my heart, Mack Sherman. I plan to write Solomon and tell him how you tried to bring the doctor when Barbara was born. Eat. Rest. Then I need you to go out to the barn. Old Prince and Molly still need you."

Forgiveness is the most blessed of all Christian virtues. This love, this care, this wiping away of all mistakes and failures. It is not humanly possible to forgive, but it is the precious touch of grace that gives such strength. They were still a family. They needed each other and all of their pitiful resources. They must walk by faith.

Soon, terror struck again. A few months before they'd been living in fear of the roving bands of desperados, thieves, and jayhawkers who thundered into the county from Kansas. So far they'd escaped, except for their cows and horses. But now it was the Southern sympathizers from Bates and Cass counties here in Missouri—the feared bushwhackers—who were wreaking havoc.

They were caught between. The jayhawkers ravaged and burned the property of the pro-Southerners. The bushwhackers plundered the property, and kidnapped, hung, or shot the Northerners caught in their raids. God help any man in the Union uniform when the dreaded bushwhackers swept down into the county.

They descended upon Sarah's farm on Tuesday, February 2. The sun had risen over a cloud bank in the east, casting a rich orange, then pink, glow. The cloud bank spread, glowering, half covering the sky. A foreboding hung in the air.

Mack heard them first. Soon a band of seventeen came

thundering across the wooden bridge. They wore their grotesque, homemade uniforms of assorted greys. While a dozen pillaged the barn, blasting holes in the roof with their rifles and dragging the bellowing Molly from her stall, the other five kicked open the kitchen door and shoved into the room. Fierce scowls wreathed their weather-scarred faces.

A gun barrel was thrust into Marianne's side.

"Lookit cheer! An ole nigger woman a livin' with 'ese 'ere whites. 'Bout time someone brings the law o' decency inta this 'ere house. Har, har, har!" The awful laugh ascended, bouncing off the wide boards of the ceiling.

At first, Marianne wanted to cower, to drop down and hang her head. Then strength mounted within her. "You git that gun outta' my ribs, you nothin' but po' white trash. This here's a Christian home. Men'nite lady and her children live here." Her strong, black hands gripped the gun barrel fearlessly as she heaved it backwards. The sorry bushwhacker, angered by her rebuke, withdrew his gun and gave her face a resounding slap with his leather glove. Then he wilted at her strength and the power of her eyes.

"God in heaven," Sarah prayed, "God in heaven, save us!" Then she remembered: "Thou shalt not be afraid for the terror by night; nor for the arrow that flieth by day."

"Take what you need, only spare us. I have a sick child," her hand pointed to the bed by the fireplace. The frightened Nancy, now fully awake, raised up, weakly. Fear masked her face, but only for a moment.

"Where is your man, woman?" The soldier was gruff and harsh. She heard him cock his gun to frighten her. Outside, sounds of the coarse jeering of the plunderers rose up. She caught only a glimpse of them as they drug her hams and smoked meats from the smokehouse.

A saddled bushwhacker held a rope that encircled Molly's neck. Again, loud hoots rose up at the flames that caught in the wind and now consumed the barn and smokehouse. Mack was rudely thrown from one leering bushwhacker to another. The poor man was petrified as they threatened to string him up on the limb of the same tree where old Barney had recently hung.

"Take what you need." She said it again, glancing over at Marianne. She hoped that Marianne would not resist and put them in further danger.

But Marianne had been over such a road many times before in her life of slavery. She was far wiser than that. She followed the example set by Sarah. She knew that if they resisted they would probably be shot and the house would be consumed in flames around them.

Marianne walked over to post herself like a sentinel to protect the pale child with the flowing yellow hair stretched out on her bed.

"You touch this child and God'll strike you dead!" She said it with such earth-shaking conviction that the ragged soldier dipped his head, half ashamedly, and halted.

Then the sergeant of the motley group, having supervised the plundering and stealing outside, burst through the door and into the room. "Hurry, we're wasting time. Leave the women and children alone. We need the bedding, the pillows, and the kitchen utensils."

He gave a command to the second ruffian to begin stripping the beds. A callous bushwhacker's foot struck the wooden cradle and little Barbara began to cry, then scream, in fright. Sarah, nearly fainting with weakness and fear, bent over and brought the frightened baby to her breast.

Approaching Nancy's bed by the fireplace, the ruffian leered as he grabbed a hold of the beautiful patchwork quilt which had been brought from Ohio. "Ain't dis 'ere sumpthin'? I'm a gonna take dis 'ere an' sleep under it with one o' 'em Yankee girls up 'ere on that hill."

The quilt, made by Nancy's grandmother, was snatched from the bed by dirty hands that had shed much blood. It was rolled carelessly and rudely into a bundle and tossed out into the kitchen where another bushwhacker was throwing together skillets, pots and pans, and any food he could take along.

Marianne had tried to stop them, but Sarah's glance told her, "Let them take it." She hollered out, "That there quilt done been made by Men'nites way out in Ohio. You take it and I'm tellin' you, God'll strike you dead!"

This time, Marianne got a heavy boot thrust into her broad backside. The kick sent her jarring against the bedstead.

Then Nancy, all the traces of fear gone from her face, sat up with some supernatural strength. Her face seemed lighter, her golden hair, a halo. Her voice was steady. "Take what you need. Do not use your tongues and bodies to harm others." Then, she remembered her friends in Christ from *Martyrs Mirror,* Mary and Anna, and their crowns of straw. She remembered how, with their persecutors taunting them, they remained faithful and honored Christ.

"Take what you need. All of us will pray for you." Then she collapsed in a faint as Sarah and Marianne rushed to her bedside.

Gathering their plunder, the bushwhackers left, quickly, silently, touched by the presence of some power beyond themselves. They lowered their eyes in guilt, slinking out to join their comrades who were by now leaping into their saddles and heading out the barnyard gate.

Mack, trembling and fear-stricken, saw a drunken soldier tip one of his apple jack jugs, take a long draft from it, then give a blood-curdling whoop and gallop off down the frozen dirt road.

When they were gone they sized up their losses. Only smoldering coals were left of the barn and smokehouse. If the wind let up and the coals died down, perhaps they could salvage bits and pieces of charred wood for the fireplace. Thank God they still had the wood stacked at the edge of the timber, but it would take strength to cut it and drag it up to the house.

Marianne yanked off her heavy woolen petticoat to cover Nancy, whose fever had been touched off by the chaos and stress. Sarah reached behind the bedroom door for her old work coat. She spread it for a blanket over Marianne's petticoat. "God, how will we survive now?" she murmured to herself.

The thieves had not noticed the opening that led down to their dug out under the back porch were she had her crock of salt pork and a few potatoes and onions. "Oh God, make it last," she prayed.

Jarred by the awful crisis, their limited resources, and Nancy's failing health, the bonds between them were strengthened. Suffering bound them closer together, turning their hearts and souls even more closely to God.

Sarah read from the Scriptures by the light of a stub of a remaining candle she'd found under the bed. "He hath given meat unto them that fear him; he will ever be mindful of his covenant."

Three days later the winter winds tore loose again. Blinding snow beat against the window. The wind mourned and howled as if it carried the weight and the sorrows of those caught up in these border wars.

That was the night Nancy died. Marianne, sleeping on a pallet on the floor by her bed, roused from her light sleep as she heard the sounds from the child's lips. Nancy was praying. Hurriedly, Marianne poked up the fire. Blazing up, it cast its orange light upon the pale face. Bending over, Marianne drew Nancy to her side with her strong arm. "Child, you needin' more of my broth? Marianne'll warm it for you."

Nancy, her thin arm reaching up to clasp Marianne's hand, looked up into the tender, loving face of her dear friend. "Oh, Marianne, I love you so. I've prayed that President Lincoln will free you and all the slaves. You know that you are free here, Marianne. You are one of us and we all are Christ's. Tell mother to come."

Lying back down, she awaited the touch of her mother's hand. "Dear, dear mother, dear father, dear darling baby sister, I love you all so."

Kneeling by her bedside, Sarah tenderly clasped the thin, failing body of her daughter to her. She did not want to weep openly, but great tears ran down her cheeks. Sarah knew that Nancy was slipping away to that unseen shore.

"Oh, dear daughter, dear, dear Nancy. Child, I love you. What more can I do?" Almost without realizing it she turned her tear-streaked face to Marianne for help, for strength. But, they both knew that the hour for attempting to search and find a doctor was already past. Like the balm of Gilead, the words from the Scripture she'd read just that evening bathed her spirit: "For we know that if our earthly house of this tabernacle were dissolved, we have a building of God, a house not made with hands, eternal in the heavens."

She could not hold back this child whom God was calling. Strange. She had tried to deny it, but hadn't she known it all along? She'd always tried to make herself believe that this child, such a gift to Solomon and to her, was really stronger than she was.

But it was the child's vital and living spirit that had bound her body to her soul these years of hers upon this earth. God had touched this child, had breathed through her. Oh, how they would miss her love. With an almost unbearable ache, Sarah laid the thin body back upon the bed and kissed the fevered cheek.

Nancy opened her eyes. "Tell father I love him so. I see ..." Her face glowed with a light not of this earth. With blue eyes opened wide, she focused upon something or someone beyond earthly boundaries. "Oh, Marianne, mother, I see ..."

Before the frail lips could utter what the eyes of the soul had seen, she died.

Chapter 16

How does one human being, suffering so many losses, find the strength to march on? Only by faith. Only by paying attention to the deepest part of the soul. Only by finding a strength that is beyond oneself, yet very near.

Grace came to Sarah in words flowing down through her mind, over and over, through the searing pain and the detached deadness of her own body. "When thou passeth through the waters, I will be with thee; and through the rivers, they shall not overflow thee."

Sarah found the strength to do first things first. She had to calm herself, sit down, head in hand, and think it through. Step-by-step. Bereaved, broken, robbed, buildings burned, mules and cows stolen, precious food dragged away ....

But first things first. There had to be a funeral to bury this angel child.

She sent Mack over the hard-packed snow to see a neighbor, Abel Sloan. She knew that Mack needed the support of a stronger man. She sent him with firm and clear instructions. "I want you to go up near Harrisonville towards that little cemetery, you know, the one with those beautiful pine trees."

Oh, yes, the pines. The wind and the pines. One could leave the body of this lovely child there, buried near such pines, but only with the help of God.

"Find out," she'd told them, "what it costs to buy a plot.

Do what you must do. Tell them that I shall pay." She only hoped that the two silver coins sewn into the lining of her coat would be enough. They'd been hiding there since the day of her baking at the hotel, long ago.

Sarah and Marianne laid out the fragile body and prepared it for burial. When the bathing was finished, and she had combed that precious hair for the last time, she kissed the pale, cold cheeks and hands.

Next, she knelt before the crude wooden chest in the corner of her bedroom. Lifting the heavy lid, she searched. There it was, the white and cream colored quilt her Aunt Mary had given her on her wedding day.

She needed it now. Yes, she'd line the homemade casket with it. She'd hoped to use it as a bedspread whenever they'd be prosperous enough to have a guest bedroom. She held it for a moment, seeing in her mind her Aunt Mary's face. She needed them now, her Ohio kinfolk. She needed the warmth, the sharing of the grief, the shedding of tears together, the sharing of the life and deeds of the one now cold in death.

And she needed the bishop and the gathering of the congregation, with its soul-moving singing and the reading of the holy words. She needed them all so that she could endure lowering Nancy's body into that awful scar in the earth. Oh, how she ached for Solomon's presence.

Thank God for Marianne. The awe-filling strength of this woman surrounded her, and mingled with her own strength and spirit. Marianne, her face shiny with glistening tears, held the infant Barbara and cooed to her.

Then Marianne, who knew the meaning and pain of shredded and broken hearts, began to murmur and sing in her vibrant, deep voice: "In the mornin' when I rise, give me Jesus!"

The blessed music swirled out into the darkness of the room, lighted only by the morning light in the small eastern window. "Give me Jesus." Grace came to Sarah Yoder through such sounds and words. Grace to do one thing at a time.

Abel Sloan and his wife, Priscilla, stomped the snow from their boots as Mack opened the porch door. Sarah would not have the comfort of a Mennonite sister, but the embrace of this English woman, whom she scarcely knew, touched her and the boundaries dissolved.

It had cost exactly two dollars to buy the tiny plot. Priscilla Sloan would stay here with Sarah and Marianne. Mack and Abel Sloan returned to the cemetery in Sloan's spring wagon, ducking their heads in the cold northeastern wind that had sprung up. They would be using the power of their muscles, shoulders, backs, and arms as they picked at the frozen earth, cracking its crust, heaving up the black soil.

They were lowly people, people of the land. It was a human thing to use one's hands and arms, the strength of one's back to dig a grave. Sarah'd do it herself for the body of her child, if she had the strength.

There was no time to send Mack all the way eastward over the hill to seek the aid of a Mennonite brother or deacon. Who knew? Maybe the raiders had plundered and killed over there and they were burying their own. Time was precious. One thing at a time. Then, she must write Solomon.

The two men, dirt covered, weary, and sore, returned just as the sun slid over a cloud bank in the west. They'd build the small coffin inside by the light of the fireplace. Sarah had shown the men five wide boards that made part of the east wall of her porch. She ran her hand over them, feeling the roughness left by their sawing. She nodded her head, then whispered, "Use these."

So the two men, saying not a word, began to knock the boards from their framing. Inside the small room, the sawing and the pounding of the iron nails into the grey soft wood was almost more than Marianne could stand. She began wailing a song of such soul-touching beauty that the men stopped hammering until she'd finished: "Oh! Mamma don't you weep for me, Mamma don't you weep for me. Oh! Watch and pray.

Mamma don't you weep for me."

The next morning they slid the small grey coffin into the back of Abel Sloan's spring wagon. Sarah and Priscilla sat on the wagon seat, while Mack steadied the coffin. They wound their way up the curving road toward the tall pines that were sighing in the wind.

Marianne, wedged between the coffin and the sideboard, held the infant, Barbara. Cold wind circled their heads and shoulders.

With the harness reins, Abel and Mack Sherman lowered the rude box into the black gash in the soiled snow. Sloan's horses stomped their feet and snorted. The pines, graced with snowflakes, bent sorrowfully in the wind.

Then Marianne, passing the infant to her mother, brushed her windswept black skirts with her ungloved hands, lifted up her tear-stained face, and began her funeral hymn: "Oh Jesus! You know our sorrow. Oh Jesus! You know our sorrow. Oh Jesus! you know our sorrow. Smile on this child, smile on this child."

It seemed as if the wind itself was aware of such a sacred hour. For a moment it stopped.

Silently Sarah stepped forward with her worn German Bible that had been passed on from mother to daughter. Her weary face was lighted only by her dark eyes glancing up, then down upon the precious page. Her lips, without falter, pronounced the words of eternal comfort: "And they brought young children to him, that he should touch them ... Jesus said unto them, 'Suffer the little children to come unto me, and forbid them not; for of such is the kingdom of heaven.'" And, "Blessed are the dead which die in the Lord from henceforth; Yea, saith the spirit, that they may rest from their labors; and their works do follow them."

She hadn't planned to do it, but when Sarah finished reading, she clutched the Bible to her black-clothed breast, lifted her bonneted head, and began singing:

> Children of the heav'nly Father
> Safely in His bosom gather;
> Nestling bird nor star in heaven
> Such a refuge e're was given.

Sarah, voice breaking at last, read the committal passage from the holy Word, giving the body to the earth and the soul to God who gave it.

Then Sarah and Priscilla climbed silently into the spring wagon, followed by Marianne and the carefully wrapped infant. Priscilla Sloan took the reins. The two men stayed behind.

The heavy snow muffled the sounds of the horse hooves and the wagon wheels. The women rocked homeward in silence, soon lost in the blanket of grey fog that engulfed them.

They were sustained by that light the gospel mentions—the light that is not overcome by the darkness.

Under the pines, outlined by the eerie light between the clouds and the ground, the two men struggled to fill the ugly gash in the earth.

Chapter 17

It took three weeks for Solomon Yoder to receive Sarah's letter bearing the agonizing news

"Oh, Nancy!" He wept. Great heaving sobs shook his body. Bent over, head in his hands, the salt tears flowed through his fingers.

He wept for Sarah and her bleeding heart, for the newborn Barbara and all of her sweet innocence thrown into this broken world that was filled with such anguish. Solomon wept for himself, for his own losses. Day by day, he'd tried to do his duty.

Relieved at last from kitchen service, his back grew weary from bending over the dying and wounded as he tried to bring them merciful comfort through his hands—binding the ragged, awful sores and wounds, holding the heads of the fevered in his lap. "Oh, God," he prayed, "Where does it lead? How shall it end?"

Solomon sought permission for a bereavement furlough from the colonel. It was denied him. He was at the edge of a great woods by the Mississippi near St. Louis. The distance was too far.

Besides, he'd been told, wasn't he the one with the sensitive conscience that had given them a headache and problems sorting out where he could do service for his country? "No. The funeral is now long past. This is the way it is in war," he'd been told.

There was a great emptiness in the little home by Grand River, an emptiness that hung like wet, dark blankets around Sarah and Marianne. How does one go on the next day and the next, after the death of a precious child?

Sarah wanted to drop everything and stop her brain from concentrating on how they would survive the months ahead. She wanted to run—no bonnet, no coat, barefooted—to the hill of the pines and throw herself at the head of that little snow-covered mound that had become sacred and holy to her.

But she did not. She knew that if she was to keep her sanity she must focus on her first duty, mothering Baby Barbara. Thank God, her milk had not dried up.

The child nursed, smacking loudly as she rocked her. Then Marianne would take the infant, lest Sarah allow herself to sit and rock throughout the day. If she allowed it, she would get a faroff gaze in her eyes, as the sorrow worked itself through her body, mind, and spirit.

If one were to ask Sarah later in her life, "How did you make it through those spring and summer months?" she would have given a solemn stare, looked up with her sorrowful dark eyes, brushed back a wisp of hair from her forehead, shaken her head, and whispered, "Grace. It was grace."

In late spring when the roads were passable, she asked Abel Sloan to drive her, Marianne, and the growing Barbara eight miles eastward over the hill to Joseph and Salome Eicher's.

One could again hear the sounds of Sarah weeping as she poured out her anguish to her people. Oh, the healing of the touch and prayers of people of her faith. It was a touch of that blessed balm of Gilead—the prayers together, the tender embrace of Sister Eicher, the eating together of bread baked by her faithful hands.

With her soul anointed and bound with the balm of Christian fellowship, she could again return to her little farm by the towering trees and place her hands, grown pale from the winter, around her hoe handle.

Throughout the land, paranoia, suspicion, and fear mounted. The mistrust that all war breeds seethed everywhere. Union commanders loosed a new campaign to drive out and imprison any Southern sympathizers in Cass and Jackson counties.

Falling into the clutches of these frenzied Union officers were a half dozen women, all Southern sympathizers. They were handcuffed, thrown into a wagon, bounced, and shaken over a rocky road until they were finally thrown into a decrepit, old stone building in the dusty, little cattle town of Kansas City.

Three Union officers were later held responsible for this imprisonment and for the border plundering: Senator Lane of Kansas, whose bands of guerrillas wreaked the greatest havoc among the Southern sympathizers; General Thomas Euwing, Jr.; and General Schofield, head of the Military District of the Border, who'd appointed Euwing.

Sarah's farm lay directly in the center of this military district's western edge. It was Senator Lane first, then General Euwing secondly, who would go down in history as responsible for the worst event of the Border Wars.

Back in the stone prison building in Kansas City, the Southern women huddled together. One was Charity Kerr, sister to the dreaded William Quantrill's chief scout. Two others were Jesse and Frank James's own mother and sister. Then, there was Josephine Anderson, sister to the cutthroat Bloody Bill Anderson, plus cousins of the outlaw Cole Younger, as well as others.

Deprived of water and food, they suffered in the condemned building, fearing for their lives. There were those who petitioned General Euwing on their behalf, but to no avail. Escape was impossible, as they were guarded around the clock by an armed Union sergeant.

Finally one hot August morning, just as early risers were walking the streets and heavy wagons began to rumble by, the decrepit building began to shake and collapse. The weight of heavy beams and stones crushed down upon the helpless women. Four were dead, the remainder, seriously wounded.

The renowned American painter, George Caleb Bingham of Arrowrock, Missouri, took it upon himself to publish in the Washington Sentinel:

> While in prison, walls were trembling, its doors remained closed, and they were allowed to hope for no release except through the portals of a horrible death.... The fact that no inquiry was instituted by General Euwing ... and no soldier punished ... renders it impossible for him to escape responsibility therefore, and also for tragedies resulting therefrom, in the deaths of hundreds of Union soldiers and citizens of Missouri, as well as the brutal massacre which immediately followed in the state of Kansas.

When the news of the death and injuries to these Southern women reached the ears of William Quantrill and his band, a vow of vengeance rose up to the heavens.

Bloody Bill Anderson, who loved nothing more than to cut throats, vowed to take the scarf from his neck and tie a knot for every person murdered in cold blood that day by the collapsing walls.

Chapter 18

"Lawsey, Miss Sarah, what's that noise?"

Marianne tossed her broom in the corner by the fireplace, her heavy body rolling as she went to the window and peered out. Cold-blooded war whoops rose up in the dust and the thunder of hooves. An eerie orange light from the setting sun softened the contours of the thundering army riding past the house.

Sarah, who'd been nursing Barbara, laid the child in her cradle and stepped briskly to Marianne's side. Her rough hand rose to her throat in fear and dread. Now what? What awful catastrophe faced them now?

"Even the score with Lane! Lawrence, Lawrence. Revenge, revenge!" yelled the bloodthirsty crew riding by.

They had selected Lawrence, Kansas, since it was the home of the hated Lane and his jayhawkers. Over one hundred fifty horses with riders plunged over the wooden bridge at the edge of Sarah's land, riding with fury like the horsemen of the Apocalypse.

The moaning of the wind through the ancient cottonwoods and oaks standing to this day, still whispers and palls at the awful events of that night, as this cutthroat band merged with Quantrill's band and over three hundred bloodthirsty guerrillas crossed the state line.

Across the twilight sky they rode, bearing the vows of

death in their hearts, greed and awful revenge leering from their eyes.

When nightfall came, they descended upon isolated, lonely Kansas farmers, kidnapping them and forcing them at gunpoint and with scandalous threats to point out the way across the ditches and rivers to the sleeping city of Lawrence.

More than ten Kansas frontier farmers lost their lives that night, as they, one by one, were discarded and shot. Along the way the awful hoards plundered and burned the farmhouses, and amidst the jeering shrieks, raped the women.

On and on they rode, this band of vile murderers, descending without warning upon the sleeping town of Lawrence.

"Mount Oread, Mount Oread," they yelled into the wind as they raced toward the high hill marking the city. The death of the fourth horseman fell upon that sleeping city that night. "Remember the murdered women of Kansas City!"

Historian Robert Townsend reports that they left eighty widows, two hundred and fifty orphans, and streets and walks filled with the dead and injured. Setting fire to the town in the early morning, William Quantrill and his deadly band left the once lovely little Kansas town a pile of smoke and ashes.

Lane, chief on their list, escaped to Missouri and safety with General Euwing. Bloody Bill Anderson rolled in blood that day, his hands were red as he took off his neck scarf to tie in fifteen new knots, each standing for a person whose throat he personally had cut.

Four days later, General Euwing issued his infamous Order Number Eleven, greatly affecting Sarah, Marianne, and all their neighbors in Cass County. It was an order that haunted him all the days of his life.

He commanded that all persons living within Jackson, Cass, and Bates counties (with a few exceptions) remove themselves from their places of residence within fifteen days. They were commanded to go to Fort Harrisonville or to

Pleasant Hill to the commanding officer of the military station to give testimony of their loyalty. When this was verified, certificates of loyalty to the Union would be issued.

All who received such certificates were then allowed to move to a military station within the district. For Sarah, this would be Pleasant Hill or Harrisonville. Those not qualifying for certificates of loyalty were told to immediately move out of the district. Officers, commanding companies, and detachments serving these counties were given orders to enforce the command with fervor.

All grains stored and within fields accessible to the military were required to be removed to serve the Union forces. All such grain and hay not brought to headquarters after September 9 would be burned and destroyed. Of the ten or twelve thousand inhabitants in Cass County, about 600 remained, seeking shelter at the military posts at Harrisonville and Pleasant Hill. The county to the south, Bates, was completely depopulated within two weeks, and remained that way for three years.

In Cass County one third of the houses were burned, and one half of the farms laid waste. Thousands of citizens in Cass and Jackson counties stood helplessly by as their houses, barns, haystacks, and fields were consumed by flames. Since the guerrilla bushwhackers responsible for the burning of Lawrence only moved southward deeper into Missouri, they were not affected at all. Only the innocent suffered.

Sarah clutched the written order tightly in her hand. Her heart froze with terror. Hadn't she suffered enough? What about Marianne, who would have been homeless without her reaching out to provide for her.

Didn't they know or care that her very own husband was in the Union army? God, what would she do? And, the farm, the land? Would it be burned?

Sarah mingled the cry of her aching heart with the countless cries of those of centuries past, who endured such pain, loss, and the burning of the land: "For unto thee, O Lord, I cry, for fire has devoured the pastures of the wilderness, and flame has burned all the trees of the field. Even the wild beasts cry to thee because the water brooks are dried up and fire has devoured the pastures of the wilderness."

Marianne's low murmurings—the deep, soul-moving songs of slaves, of pain and hardship, of hope and faith—drew her back inside the house. Their future now was unknown.

Chapter 19

Since the dastardly raid by the bushwhackers just before Nancy's death, Sarah had no grain—neither corn, wheat, nor oats. Their only farm animal was poor blind-in-one-eye Old Prince, and he was sinking daily closer and closer to the earth. He had been turned out to forage in the ten acres of corn stubble. His ribs looked like barrel stays with canvas stretched over them.

"Lawsey, Miss Sarah, what are we gonna do now?" Marianne's eyes opened in fear.

Sarah, spooning a mouthful of soft porridge into Baby Barbara's mouth, looked up. "We'll have to go. If they'll take us up to Fort Harrisonville, we'll go there. If they are too crowded, or we are turned away, God help us, we'll have to somehow try the fifteen miles to Pleasant Hill."

Sarah was thin and tired. How would she find the strength? Who would save them? Last evening, she'd released Mack. She could not pay nor feed him. He'd been nagging her to leave ever since his night spent in Red Indian Saloon. For the past three days, three Indians, two men and one woman, had been camping down by the river bend. She knew that Mack had been down there.

When she nodded her permission, Mack spat some tobacco juice, hunkered up his shoulders, and headed through the cornstalks toward the Indians and their camp, swinging his last jug of apple jack in the crook of his finger.

The next morning Mack and his companions left for Oklahoma Territory. She couldn't blame anyone for wanting to leave this war-torn country. No. If she could, she'd leave too.

"And, Marianne, you needn't call me Miss Sarah. Just plain old Sarah'll do. Aren't we Christian sisters?"

"Yes, Miss Sarah, I know I don't have to call you Miss Sarah. But I'm old, and I forget. Makes no difference 'bout President Lincoln passin' out that proclamation. I know I'll be free someday. This is my home. Ain't it?"

With tears in her eyes Sarah walked over to Marianne and gave her a warm embrace, kissing her on the cheek. "Yes, Marianne, this is your home. We are Christian sisters. Your faith strengthens mine. You saved my life, dear Marianne. I love you. But, we have to go. I fear the plunderers will come in a day or two. We have to flee for our lives. I'm certain this house will be burned to the ground."

"Miss Sarah, wherever you go, this old black body goes. I'm gonna be like Miss Ruth in the Bible."

Ruth in the Bible. The picture of love and hope that binds two sisters in faith together. Who has failed to remember the blessed words of Ruth? "Intreat me not to leave thee, or to return from following after thee; for whither thou goest, I will go; and where thou lodgest, I will lodge; thy people shall be my people, and thy God my God."

For the past two days, the roads had borne the weight of the walkers, mostly women, and the broken-down old carts and wagons that wobbled by carrying the aged, the infirm, and the little children who could not walk to Fort Harrisonville.

Sarah knew time was running out. How glad she was that when Nancy died, she'd also sent a letter to Solomon's brother, C.P. Yoder, out in Ohio. Her letter told him of their trials, their losses, and also of their faith to persevere, with God helping them.

The next morning, Marianne corralled Old Prince from

the cornstalks with the bridle she and Sarah had made for him out of some small pieces of rope. The makeshift harness they'd patched together would make any horse hee and haw. But these were desperate times, and these two women were intent on survival.

"You come here, old Marianne's got the corn for you." She'd picked up a nubbin, half hidden under a stalk, thrusting it forward on Old Prince's good side. His ears pitched forward, he neighed, then staggered forward for the handout.

Slowly, Marianne half dragged the mangy old horse toward the back of the house. He stood, still grinding on the nubbin of corn with his few worn teeth. He was glad for human companionship. He waited patiently for whatever fate dished out to him.

Inside, Sarah surveyed her remaining belongings. They only had that rickety cart. She'd have to leave most of her household furnishings. What to take? The bentwood willow rocker, the Dutch oven, the pitiful little sacks of cornmeal and flour she had left?

Then there was the cradle Solomon had made for Nancy so many years back. She'd keep that treasure as long as she could. She wrapped their clothing in the only two blankets the bushwhackers hadn't taken. Oh yes, her clock. She'd try to take the old-fashioned eight-day mantle clock from her Grandfather King back in Ohio. Clutching the worn leather Bible and the *Martyrs Mirror,* she wrapped them tenderly in a fourth of a torn flannel sheet.

She included Solomon's letters with the two heavy volumes. Tears began to slide down her cheeks as she surveyed her home—the home that had been blessed with laughter, happiness, prayers, and songs for awhile. A home that had known also the weight of sorrow and affliction, the awful pain of the death of a child.

Sarah, straightening the two bundles in her arms, headed for the edge of the back porch where Marianne struggled with the pitiful looking cart. Old Prince, head dipped, stood in front of the makeshift contraption that would hook him to it.

"Marianne, let me help." Sarah placed the heavy bundles in the cart.

"Lawsey, Miss Sarah, that old wheel ain't gonna stay on. I'm gonna fix it." She hit the bent bolt that held the wheel over the axle with a heavy stone. When it flew loose, she picked it up.

Bending over, she hammered it with her stone over a flat rock to straighten it. Then she replaced the bolt, serving as a pin to hold the wheel on the axle. Still, the wheel leaned tragically.

"Lawdy, how're we gonna make it with this here wheel leanin' like it got the stomachache?" She threw down her rock, puzzled, but not giving up.

"It'll have to do, Marianne. Hurry, time's running out. I need help with the cradle."

It'd taken them only a few minutes to load up the pitiful belongings. Looking up, Sarah noticed a black cloud spreading in the west. They'd better be heading off now, joining the stragglers and wanderers on the road to Fort Harrisonville. God only knew what faced them at the fort.

Sarah was afraid of uniforms and military men. Marianne was frightened too. President Lincoln's proclamation did not mean that she was free from harm here in this border state. But, with her prayers and the low humming of her spiritual songs, she'd face it all with Sarah.

Sarah took the worn ropes, slapping them on Old Prince's back. The journey began. The cart groaned, leaned, and wobbled. Would they make it? Marianne held the infant Barbara, who cooed and laughed at the rocking ride.

About a mile and a half down the dusty road, Old Prince stopped, his sides heaving. He looked back at his friends in the cart, then hung his head, nearly falling asleep.

"We'd better let him rest, Marianne. Don't worry. Isn't it a wonder that Barbara enjoys the ride so much?"

Had it not been for the onslaught of the war and tragedy at their heels, Sarah herself would have enjoyed the beauty of the day, and would have practically gone into hysterics laughing at the pitiful cart, its rickety ride, and especially the horse. She did allow herself a smile which covered her fears for a moment.

Jarring Old Prince out of his sleep, they crept ahead. The wheel now made a threatening noise—grinding, squeaking. Sarah had her doubts as to whether they would make it up the long hill at Fort Harrisonville. But they could put Barbara in her crib and get out and push, couldn't they?

Ahead, a wagon had broken down. Three women strained as they tried to unload two rocking chairs by the edge of the road. The wheel had fallen off completely, the axle dragging. Thank God. An old man and a stout woman just ahead of them stopped and returned to help the women. And, did you see the team pulling that wagon?

"Ain't that a sight!" cried Marianne. "Why that's just like mixin' the eggs with the apples." She chuckled in a deep contralto as her eyes rolled, surveying the poor farm women's team, one pitiful calf, and one lonely ox, sides heaving.

Maybe it was a blessing that the wind caught the dust that enveloped these beggarly wanderers and clouded other eyes from such sights—these stricken ones, broken, some aged and ill, hungry, and now, homeless.

But remember that once long ago, a lonely forsaken one, bruised in body, agonized on a stone road leading up a hill. He reminded us that "blessed are the poor, the poor in spirit." Marianne and Sarah were poor in things and poor in spirit.

Chapter 20

Both Sarah and Marianne got out of the dilapidated cart and pushed from the rear while Old Prince strained, mostly to keep himself from going to sleep until they reached the top of the hill leading into the town.

The famed artist, Bingham, took his pen and wrote of this tragic day: "I was present ... when the order was being enforced ... and can affirm from personal observation, that the sufferings of its unfortunate victims, in many instances, were such as should have elicited sympathy from hearts of stone .... It is well known that men were shot down in the very act of obeying the order, and their wagons and effects seized by their murderers."

Strangely enough, the mingling crowds were silent. The only sounds rising up were the sounds of the commanding Union officers, horses neighing, and the mooing of the oxen.

A group of rough soldiers carrying out Euwing's orders leered and shouted as they swung their rifles. They pointed and yelled confusing commands amid the swirling mass of women, old men, and crying children.

"Mercy, what are we gonna do?" Marianne grabbed Sarah's arm protectively. "I ain't gonna let them hurt you, Miss Sarah." But her eyes were glazed with fear, the old fear that forever lurks at the edge of consciousness in the heart of a slave.

They could go no farther because of the line of carts and wagons. Besides, Old Prince was near collapse.

Sarah pulled her sunbonnet forward to protect her eyes from the light, searching for someone she knew, someone who might help them face this unknown.

She caught a glimpse of Anna Eicher, the Dunker woman from over the hill. Her dark bonnet and black shawl set her apart in the crowd. A moment of joy filled her heart—others of like faith were here. They would find each other.

But before Sarah could break through the crowd to the Dunker sister, rough commands were shouted down to her from a red-whiskered, red-faced soldier, seemingly enjoying his task of goading people. He threatened them with his rifle while his comrades unloaded the carts of these unfortunate ones who'd made the mistake of gathering before them.

Sarah had hoped to get to the office where she was commanded to declare her loyalty. Instead, both she and Marianne were stopped dead here. Barbara began to cry.

"Well now," leered the red-faced soldier, spitting his brown tobacco juice at her feet, "ain't this here somethin'? An old nigger woman holdin' onto this here white woman."

His coarse laugh ascended, his body swayed from his command post atop a wagon. His comrades, obviously fortified for their tasks by hard liquor, leaned into Sarah's cart, lifting out the willow rocker.

Crash! It sailed onto a huge pile with the furniture of the unfortunates ahead of them. Next would be the cradle.

"Stop. My Bible, my Bible!" Sarah, risking the gun barrel pointing down at her, leaned into the back of the cart to drag out her Bible and her dear *Martyrs Mirror* wrapped in the torn sheet. Rough hands grabbed her by the shoulders.

"You step over there. These things ain't yours anymore." The foul breath of the poorly-trained soldier blasted her face, as she heard the crash of Baby Barbara's cradle upon the pile of abandoned furniture. Terrified, Sarah stood. Who could help her?

"Ain't that old nigger woman a slave? You're Southern. Hey, Buford, we got us a couple Southerners." He dug at poor Marianne's side with his rifle barrel.

"Oh, God." Sarah breathed. "Oh, God, help us." She wouldn't even have a chance to explain. Who would listen in this crowd and this confusion of war?

Shouts rose up. There was the crack of rifle fire over to the left. A man lay dead, shot through the forehead. His screaming wife bent over him.

Just then a sniveling, dirty soldier burst through the crowd surrounding Marianne and Sarah. Hate clouded his face, the hate brought on by war and disobedience, lust and greed. The evils of war had overtaken him.

Pointing up at the officer on the wagon he shouted, "This here's that old nigger slave woman what done for that Confederate officer out there on that hill over west!" He grabbed Marianne, pulling roughly.

"But she lives with me. She works out her room and board. Oh, I plead, don't harm Marianne." Sarah couldn't help the tears. She rocked Barbara tightly in her bosom. Oh God, who would help?

But before Sarah could say more, or anyone else come to their aid, Marianne herself rose up like Moses out of Egypt. "Let us go. We're on our way to declare our ..."

Before she could finish the sentence, another rifle shot rang out. "That'll shut up your old nigger mouth!" leered the blood-soiled soldier. A great cry of dismay rose up from those around Sarah as the ponderous body of Marianne, born down in Mississippi as a slave, who'd lived all her years as a slave, fell to the bricks beneath her.

Shock beyond belief swept over Sarah, who pushed through to her fallen friend's side. Mercifully, a tired and fear-ridden woman reached out and took the child from Sarah's arms.

She knelt, taking Marianne's red-bound head in her lap. "Oh, Marianne. Oh, Marianne," she sobbed.

Crimson blood began to soil Marianne's dress where the bullet had pierced her breast. Blood spread across the hard bricks. "Oh, Marianne, don't die." Then, looking up in pity, she cried, "Can't someone help? Is there a doctor?"

She touched the dear face with her kisses; her salt tears ran down Marianne's face. "Oh, Marianne, I love you."

Sarah rocked Marianne's body as she would rock a child. Marianne, opening her eyes, smiled with her thick lips. A great peace came over her face. "Miss Sarah, I love you too, we're sisters in the Lawd." Then her eyes closed and if you listened closely as Sarah rocked her, you could hear the low rumbling in her throat as she began to sing: "Ah tol'e Jesus it would be all right if he changed my name. Ah tol'e Jesus it would be all right if he changed my name."

Then Marianne fell into the arms of Jesus.

In shock, not knowing now what to do, Sarah reached for her baby. Weakly, she stood. A dazed blankness spread across her face. A man's hand touched her shoulder. "Sarah, Sarah Yoder. I've been looking for you." She turned faintly, seeing the pale face of a tall man dressed in the plain garb of her people of Ohio. Who was it? She couldn't make it out.

"Sarah, it's me. Christian P. Yoder." Sarah's mind reeled as she tried to sort through the awful events waterlogging her mind. C.P. Yoder? Her brother-in-law from Ohio? She couldn't put it together just yet. There was too much.

The firm and gentle hands guided Sarah and her baby through the crowd. Behind, Marianne' body was laid by the Union deputies in charge alongside others who had fallen on that tragic day trying to obey the infamous Order Number Eleven.

C.P. handed a small roll of bills to the officer. "Bury her properly," he said. "You can see how it is, I have to get this woman out of here."

Brother-in-law, C.P. Yoder, guided Sarah and the infant to a waiting wagon at the northern edge of town. Hurrying, he half dragged Sarah, taking a shortcut through the brush and trees.

Stumbling into the clearing, Sarah saw a small covered wagon. Sitting on the wagon bench, a tense look of worry on his face, hunched a soldier in the soiled grey of the rebel army. C.P. had hired this rebel prisoner to take them as speedily as possible the thirty miles to Independence.

There, another surprise awaited Sarah. In a makeshift hospital lay Solomon, weak and fevered. In his pocket was his honorable discharge from the Union army. He had served his time. As soon as possible, C.P., an angel of mercy sent of God, would take them by train back to Ohio.

Over the verdant land, great fires burned. Smoke swept up over the fields as the animals fled. Desolate and barren, the chimneys stood, solitary sentinels to tragedy and death. The wind, lonely and chill, whispered the names of the dead lying beneath the sod.

Chapter 21

The light of spring shone upon the earth like the face of Christ smiling upon them. Sarah and Barbara Yoder stood in the soft fertile loam. The war was long past.

Sarah raked the hoe with sweeping strokes as the rich soil opened for the seed beans. Her faded calico dress whipped about her legs in the wind.

Barbara, now thirteen, lifted her feet. Barefooted like her mother, her young body swayed back and forth as she dropped the shiny beans from her hand.

Some would say that she was a plain child, this Barbara. But if you looked closely, the broad forehead crowned with coal black hair was highlighted by her dark eyes, open with wonder and glistening like pools in the morning sun.

Like her mother, Barbara was intoxicated with the earth, the trees, the opening buds of the spring flowers.

Noah, her happy brother of five, played on the back porch steps with the yellow cat, Grant, named after the new president, Ulysses S. Grant, who brought the wounded nation toward healing and peace.

Salome, their yellow-haired sister of eleven, trailed behind their father, Solomon, as he followed his horses pulling the plow down the furrow.

"Mother, tell me about our place by Grand River, and about old Marianne." Barbara threw back her blue sunbonnet and cast her dark eyes up into her mother's face where the wisps of greying hair caught in the wind.

"Oh, child. Those years are long past now. Marianne loved us. She especially loved you, born on such an awful night."

Sarah's soul had healed from the weight of sorrow at Nancy's death. Both she and Solomon sat down after the war and opened their bleeding hearts to God. They could not live with bitterness. They read the Scriptures about the loving Jesus and how he, hanging on the cross, prayed, "Father, forgive them, for they know not what they do," and followed the example of their Lord.

They and many others had come back to Missouri, to the rich land where the winds sighed and the prairies opened.

First they had gathered, these Mennonites and a few of the Dunkers, and built themselves a little church at the forks of Clearfork Creek. Here Solomon Yoder and four others of his faith who had worn Union uniforms in the world's most ghastly war came forward, asking for forgiveness.

The Hartzlers, other Yoder families, Sharps, Kauffmans, Greasers, Troyers, Kings, and others all stood up in the little white meetinghouse and gazed with compassion on these five who'd returned from the war.

They could not judge their brethren; but they did feel the call of Christ to offer their forgiveness. Which one among them had not sinned during that bloody period? Which one had not compromised in some way? Then they were blessed by the communion they had together, that feast of love which binds us closer to Christ.

Noah, a fair child like his sister Nancy, ambled down the bean row with the cat in his arms. "Mother, tell us again where Nancy was buried."

Sarah caught the chubby child as he dropped Grant. She swept down to kiss his cheek. "She's buried by a tree, Noah, a beautiful pine tree. Barbara remembers, because we stopped there when we came back from Ohio. You were too small to remember."

A pine tree, forever sighing in the wind, whispering prayers and the names of those lying beneath. Sarah could now live with this death. God had given her and Solomon these other three.

And this farm, this land with its creek and trees. She must not show too much excitement over it. But it had given her great joy when she and Solomon bought it together. They finished the buildings and began tilling the land. They still owed seven hundred dollars on it, but with good weather and crops like last season, they'd get that paid off in no time. The land itself helped their healing.

"It's twelve miles away, child. Over that way." Sarah pointed westward toward the billowing clouds. "We'll hitch Dink and Sam to the wagon this fall when the crops are in and take a day to drive over there toward Harrisonville. We'll sit where she's buried. If you listen carefully, you can hear the pine tree praying and singing in the wind."

The child, satisfied with the kiss and reassuring words of his mother, followed the yellow cat back to the porch steps.

After planting four long rows of string beans, Barbara grew tired. Sweat dripped from her dark brow. She wiped her sweaty face with her arm as she turned to Sarah. "Mother, it isn't fair. Salome is out there having all that fun following after father. I'm going to get her to come and help."

Salome and Barbara were sisters, but they were not alike. One was dark, one was fair. Three years separated them. One was a "daddy's girl" who followed her father as much as she could, preferring the outside and the barn to the house and housework. Barbara was happiest when she was rolling out pie dough, emptying into her pie shell a quart of home-canned gooseberries picked from their woods.

When she heard her mother tell about Marianne's soda biscuits, she even learned how to make them all by herself.

And the house. She took as much interest in it as her mother. It wasn't fancy, but it was a sturdy four-room house, and already father and mother were talking about the time ahead when they'd have enough money to add an upstairs. She agreed with her mother that it was a fine farm and a good house.

Sarah had taken the lead, guiding Solomon to buy here, right in the middle of the Mennonites. No longer would they be lonely way over beyond Kohler Hill. They would be here with neighbors of the same precious faith, plowing, gardening, harvesting, and best of all, worshiping together.

Besides, Sarah could not live on that land left burnt and barren by the bushwhackers and rebels who brutalized them and stole their goods.

No. Better leave it behind. Here on this land, purchased at forty dollars per acre, she and Solomon started again. She finished planting the beans as she remembered their conversation last night. Solomon worried her since he came back from the war.

"I didn't think we could start again," Solomon had spoken tiredly. He sagged into a wooden chair and bent over to take off his rough boots.

"We can do it, Solomon," she had said. "Together, we'll work on it. I'm strong, and we have the children." She knew the land would be part of Solomon's healing. He needed the land.

She was worried though. She could hardly think about how he looked: eyes dark and sunken, terrible fever, little flesh hanging from his bones, racked by a terrible cough. She had to admit he was better, but still she worried. Would he even have the strength for all the work waiting to be done?

She'd helped him with the chores that night. Dragging behind old Dink and Sam, she saw that he was almost too tired to remove their harness.

"Girls, bring in the cows. You can do the milking tonight." Sarah began removing the harness from the hungry horses as Salome grabbed the copper pail and sallied forth.

Barbara sauntered slowly after, a little resentful, as she was planning to roll the dough for the blackberry cobbler. Now she'd miss out. Still she wanted to be an obedient child, as Preacher Kenagy had urged them to be. Wasn't that the way also to live long upon the land? Why, it was one of the commandments. She held her feelings and headed for the cow barn. She worried, too. When would father get better?

He'd coughed so hard that he had to interrupt his evening prayer at the table. A silence hung in the air. Little Noah climbed out of his chair and crept over to his father's side, patting his leg as if to help heal him.

When they were alone after supper, Sarah brought it up. She had to. She could not go on like this. She loved him too much, and the children and she needed him.

"Solomon, we're caught up on the plowing and gardening. We're hitching up the spring wagon and heading in to East Lynne tomorrow to see the doctor. Your cough is worse." She walked over to place her broad palm against his forehead. Yes, the fever had come on again. She could tell he could scarcely sit in the chair.

He had resisted at first. He would have preferred the healings of some one like Marianne and her herbs and potions. Marianne, however, was long dead, buried in that pauper's ground out at the edge of Harrisonville. "Ah, God, what can I do?" he half prayed, silently. It was so hard for Solomon to admit to himself how ill he was.

"Tomorrow we'll go." His reply, weak and soft, surprised her. In her heart she prayed, "Oh, thank you, Jesus."

Since it rained, Solomon couldn't plow anyway. It was a good day to ride through the soft mud the three and a half miles to East Lynne.

"East Lynne," Sarah thought to herself. What a pretty name for such a ramshackle village! But, there were a general store, a train depot, a bank, a livery stable, and a doctor in

East Lynne. Thank God. Dr. Slayden would know what to do to cure her husband.

Pale and wearied, Solomon guided the horses down the street, trying to avoid the ruts filled with water and the ducks and geese wandering about. Here and there, villagers picked their way through the mud.

While tying the horses to the hitching post, Solomon again bent over with one of his coughing spells. His thin body shook. He took the fresh handkerchief from his pocket to wipe the spittle from his lips. Blood. There were flecks of blood on the white cloth.

He tried to slip the handkerchief quickly into his pocket before Sarah could see it, but her quick dark eyes spotted the red flecks. Her heart sank. She took his arm, guiding him toward the porch.

They needed the doctor, that was for sure. Old Doctor Slayden might just as well have been named Doctor Shakyknees considering how he trembled and shook. He was a frontier doctor, advanced in age.

Hard times and much pain was etched upon his long face edged off at the chin by a scruffy white beard. He tapped Solomon's thin chest with his bony fingers. He put his ear against the warm flesh, listening to the thump of Solomon's heart and the ragged wheezing of his lungs. Solomon bent double with a wracking cough. Sarah stared at the doctor's face, searching anxiously.

"Ahem. Ahem." The doctor straightened his weary body. His eyelids drooped, then opened, as he focused them upon the waiting pair.

"Mr. Yoder," he cleared his throat and spat into the tarnished brass spittoon in the dirty corner, "you've got tuberculosis. Can't stay here. You oughta' leave this minute for the mountains if you gonna live, that is any time a' tall."

He'd given it to Sarah and Solomon straight on, right between the eyes. No pussyfooting around here. Besides, the shabby waiting room outside was filling up. A crying child howled and sobbed.

"Mountains? Where are the mountains around here?" Sarah was already searching for an answer. She expected Solomon to say, "Oh pshaw, it ain't nothin'," and wave his big hand downward in an attempt to handle the tragic message he'd been given.

"Lady, get the food into him. Shove it in. Better get a hired man to do the plowin,' this man ain't gonna do any more this season."

Chapter 22

Sarah Yoder froze for a moment, grabbing Solomon's arm which hung loosely in his blue sleeve. But Sarah Yoder had been used to hard knocks, cold winds, guerrilla bands holding her up, guns pointed at her. She'd endured the agony of Solomon's long absence, going off to war like that. Nancy's death, the murder of dear old Marianne, all of it and more.

Yes, if ever there were a woman prepared for bad news, it was Sarah Yoder. A strength from beyond herself rose up, a strength felt by many other of her frontier sisters, who, with their husbands, were trying to build homes at the edge of the prairie.

Her firm fingers encircled her husband's arm tenderly. "The mountains, where are the mountains?" Her brains searched. Oh, yes, out west. Way out west. Wasn't it Colorado?

Other Mennonites had already made the journey there. God only knows where they landed, or what happened to them." How on earth would Solomon Yoder get to the mountains in Colorado? He might as well have mentioned the moon.

Dink and Sam, glad to be heading home for a scoop of oats, hardly noticed the slimy mud at all. The wagon rolled with easy lurch, almost without sound.

"Ain't a' gonna do it. I'll get over this come hot weather, you only need to ..." but a wracking cough cut off his words.

"Give me the reins, Solomon." Worry lined her dark face.

She mustn't let him see her fear. She knew he ought to be lying down in the back of the wagon. Thank God the rain had stopped. "We'll get you there, Solomon. Some way, God help us, we'll get you there. I'll go right away and talk this over with C.P."

But, Solomon didn't want his brother C.P. to be involved in this. Weren't they indebted to C.P. Yoder enough already? A brother who'd rescued them from the flames of the border war?

Well, C.P. had been foolish enough to catch the spirit of the west and move back here with them, along with his wife, Leah, and his children, Ben and Ike and Elizabeth. They were busy making bricks for the big square house they were building over southwest through the woods. Don't get Brother C.P. any more involved in their lives.

But Sarah did. After she'd put Solomon to bed, fevered and chilling, she'd worked with Barbara, stirring up a big kettle of beef stew. Then she baked fresh bread. "You'll need to watch your father. Don't let him get up. I'm going to ride old Dink over to Uncle C.P.'s. Should be back by evening. Start the milking, Barbara, if I'm not back in time. Mind Noah, Salome." She'd try to keep as much of this worry from the children as she could.

She hadn't thought about it—being alone on that horse to and from Uncle C.P.'s—the silence, the rhythm of the horse's body and feet, the cold wind whipping about her neck. Still, how nice it was, and how being alone like that helped her get it all sorted out.

Uncle C.P. came right to the point. "We'll send him west, Sarah. I've got plenty of help here. I can hire Widow Anna Hartzler's boy if I need more. It would help her out. Ben's sixteen and dyin' to see the west. Gonna send Ben with the spring wagon. He'll take Solomon across the prairie. Yes, that oughta' be healing for anybody, riding across the prairie, let alone the mountains. Gonna get to them mountains myself some of these days. Gotta house to build right now."

"Oh, blessed God above!" Sarah rejoiced. Riding back in the twilight, stumbling along on the back of old Dink, she prayed. God soothed her burning soul with those eternal words of comfort, "He will not suffer thy foot to be moved; he that keepeth Israel shall neither slumber nor sleep."

Then she saw herself in the meetinghouse, prayer veiled, grouped with the sisters in prayer and singing:

> O love divine that stooped to share
> Our sharpest pang, our bitt'rest tear,
> On thee we cast each earth-born care,
> We smile at pain while thou art near.

It was the singing together that healed her wounds the most. They must not miss meeting together, no matter what. Blessed Christ, who reached forth to the multitudes, if he were only present with Solomon now, he'd stretch out his nail-pierced hand and heal.

He was present. He was in the heart of every believer, even a humble farmer like Solomon. Thank God for the presence of Christ.

Sarah turned into the barnyard and headed old Dink toward the stable. She had good news for Solomon. She'd pack his things tomorrow.

Chapter 23

Four-thirty. Time to get up. Sarah's body rose to the occasion. There wasn't time to think about whether or not she felt like it. Who could take time for such luxury? There was work to be done. Today she planned to help the girls shovel the manure out of the cow barn and spread it on the field where they'd harvested the oats.

Looking at her lean frame in the light of the kerosene lamp, she gave little thought to the grey hair she pulled through the comb. Giving it a few sweeps, she wound it in the back, then pinned it in her usual bun, high off the nape of her neck.

A body needs all the air circulating around the neck it can get in this hot weather. "Well, what do you expect at forty-nine?" Sarah thought to herself.

Maybe she had begun to look a bit grandmotherly and worn, the wrinkles at the corners of her eyes, those lines running down by her nose, furrows in her brow.

She twisted her hair and sliced through it with her pins. Well, worn though she may look, they planned to make it—Barbara, Salome, Noah, and she. She couldn't yet say that the pain was gone from Solomon's dying.

Thank God he didn't have to struggle for breath anymore. In that way death was merciful. Filling the day with the work of the hands and arms, the bending, aching back, the bursting of the brains trying to figure out how they would pay the mortgage on the land—it all helped to drown the sorrow and fill the emptiness.

Other sisters in the church had lost their husbands, too. Three infants had died of scarlet fever the past winter. She hadn't lost any time at all hurrying to these heartbroken mothers. Hadn't God prepared her?

She blew out the lamp and hurried to the garden to hoe the tomatoes before the sun came up. Like a blessing from God, the cool morning wind flowed over her, bringing courage for the day.

She'd read from her Bible later while she had her morning coffee. Now, she could open herself to this thing called life, its mystery, its bundle of anguish, joy, sorrow, and laughter.

Thoughts of the summer of '75 and Solomon, cold in death, overtook her. Who would want to relive that summer? Maybe it was part of the healing, calling to mind that tragic year.

She couldn't help but think of the words of the psalmist, "O my God, my soul is cast down within me: therefore will I remember thee ... the Lord will command his lovingkindness in the daytime, and in the night his song shall be with me."

The words she'd shared with neighbor Anna Troyer floated to the top of her brain, hanging there. Yes, the summer of '75 would never be forgotten.

The Troyers, Anna and Frank, had ridden over in their spring wagon after the avalanche of grasshoppers to see how Sarah and the children had survived.

"Why, they et up Frank's britches, all 'twas left was them metal buckles," Anna said as he opened her blue eyes wildly, still in terror of the ghastly insects.

One of the reasons Solomon had consented to heading out west with Nephew Ben was because the crops were all in the ground and looked promising. Spring rains had come. Sarah and the two girls, big enough now to do a day's work, plus Ezra Swick, who had promised to come over and give a helping hand twice a week, could handle the work. Things looked promising enough, even to a sick man.

Sarah knew that others in the church were praying for them, and had offered their work-worn hands to give assistance when they could. Thank God for a church, for a community.

Folks said the grasshoppers laid their eggs in western Missouri in the spring of 1874 after taking a big swath through the Dakotas all the way down to northern Texas.

Just about when Solomon and Ben Yoder were crossing the Smokey Hill River, way out west in Kansas, Barbara had come running, screaming, "Mother. A storm, a storm!"

She hadn't noticed it yet, caught up as she was in trying to get old Dink to turn around at the corner of her garden where she was doing a little plowing. Salome yanked the harness, trying to get Dink to step forward.

Then she heard it. Rumbling like thunder, yet not thunder. Over in the west, the sky grew black. It was if someone had a large canvas that stretched from the western horizon to the edges of the earth, pulling it forward over the sky.

"Unhook Dink." Whatever kind of storm this was, they'd try to get Dink in the barn.

"Oh Mother ..." Before the frightened Salome could utter another word, what seemed like black hail rained down upon them.

In only a few minutes, it was almost as black as night as the sun clouded over from the swarming hoards.

"Bugs! Bugs! Oh, Mother, bugs! Salome screamed as she began to scrape the grasshoppers out of her face and hair with her flailing arms.

Almost freezing in her terror, Sarah could only think of her green corn, up two feet already, popping and stretching daily. And the wheat. Oh, God, the wheat, let alone the garden and the pasture.

"Run Barbara, run, close the windows and doors." But, her voice was lost in the pelting of the insects upon the ground, the trees, the roofs of the house, smokehouse, and shed.

Old Dink went crazy, as did the other pitiful creatures caught in the onslaught. The farm animals bleated, neighed, mooed, and cackled in terror. Blinded, they ran in circles, bumped into each other, piled up in fence corners.

Over west, the Aaron Hartzlers—all five of them—began to plow a ditch around their field of green wheat. Three of the boys swept hoards of grasshoppers into the ditch. "Run, get kerosene. We'll burn them," hollered Father Hartzler. But to no avail. There was no way to stop the plague of grasshoppers.

Mable Heatwole, walking by the edge of the woods east of Camp Branch, was coming home from selling her basket of eggs at Gunn City when the grasshoppers came. She threw up her empty basket and her purse to the wind, forgetting her money. She ran, she screamed, she cried to God.

They say Old Mable lost her mind that day when the grasshoppers started swarming up under her dress and crawled by the thousands under her sleeves. They found her the next day in the bend of Camp Branch, hunching in the water, addled and crazed, not even knowing her name or where she belonged.

There went the crops. Salome didn't get the wash off the line quickly enough, and their underdrawers, hanging out in the May air, hung in shreds and ribbons.

It wouldn't have been so bad if the plague had blown in and blown out. Some damage, yes. But the grasshoppers kept coming. From May 15 until June 15 they swarmed, laid eggs, gnawed the bark of trees, hoe handles, straw hats, drove animals crazy, consumed from the earth every green blade of grass, every vegetable top, the windswept blades of wheat and oats, stalks and green, sap-filled leaves of corn. Everything.

For thirty days, the grasshoppers kept coming. Sarah would sweep and shovel them off the porch, turn around, and the floor would be covered again.

"The hogs, the hogs, we'll feed them to the hogs."

So Salome, Barbara, and Noah filled the apple baskets

full of the squirming masses. They heaved them over the fence rail into the roughhewn trough, but the hogs couldn't keep up. It was futile. A pall hung over the land.

Farmers, attempting to burn scattered hay and fodder, ringed their fields with fire. But how long could they keep such fires burning? Tomorrow the hordes would descend again. Kansas City, depending upon the produce of the surrounding farmers, organized a relief society to dispense aid to the ruined farm families.

On May 17, Governor Hardin proclaimed June 3 as a day of fasting and prayer. Sarah and her brood of three looked like war refugees as they drove old Dink and Sam through the smoky haze, the bare landscape, and trees scraped of green.

Silently they gathered in the little meetinghouse. Their murmured prayers seemed feeble and halting. But they were offered from afflicted and bruised hearts. They were again reminded that as frontier farmers, they depended on a Power greater than themselves. There was no certainty on this earth: war, pestilence, death, and the threat of famine made the exalted humble.

As Sarah and her three growing youngsters lit the lamp at evening, no longer could they smile with joy and think of the rich harvest of corn and wheat, the canned and dried vegetables and fruits stored away.

Like their neighbors around them, they racked their brains for ways to survive. There would be joyful news for father when he returned, hopefully in better health from his long journey. No filled corn cribs, no fat hogs, just an empty basement. Could they even keep the animals alive?

"Mother, can't we plant corn again?" Noah was a sturdy and brave lad, longing to stand behind the plow like his father. "We still have some corn on the cob in the crib."

"We have a loft full of that old dried hay on the west side of the barn, Mother. We can keep the milk cows goin' on that. Won't give much milk, maybe, but maybe the pastures will soon green up," Salome said, consolingly.

"Couldn't we get some of Uncle C.P.'s leftover garden seeds and try again with a garden? I'll work extra hard." We all know Barbara Yoder loved a garden. Have to forget any flowers though, this year, but maybe some turnips later this fall.

Sarah had done it before, plowing. It made her weary and her shoes filled with the crumbling soil. It was better this way, though. Plowing, then harrowing, the reins pulling her arms, jerking her body, the scorching heat pouring down upon her, the westerly winds, now arisen, whipping her sleeves and skirt.

Hard work, weariness, slave-like toil. Sunup till sundown and then some. She hadn't known she had it in her. Barbara, turning fourteen, took the plow handles and clucked her tongue at the ragged team so her mother could rest in the shade cast by the tree trunk—not the leaves—for they were just emerging again, tender, hesitant.

Noah and Salome sat in the oppressive heat of the corn crib, shelling by hand the remaining nubbins set aside for replanting. It might be too late, but they would try. Sarah put lard on their blistered palms, come evening.

Then, the blessed earth greened again, coaxed on by the sweeping, summer rains. Sarah's crooked rows showed promise—green shoots, tender stalks, then husks of hanging corn, late, of course, but better than none. Her fall garden blessed them with promise, where the earlier one had vanished. And on September 17, Solomon Yoder came riding down the lane.

Noah spotted him first. The mule team, weary, but recognizing home, lifted their heads and quickened their steps.

"Mother. Father's comin'. Father's comin' down the lane!" His bare feet pounded the porch boards as he leaped off, tearing over the yard and down the lane. Sarah ran too. Her body, hardened by toil, leaned ahead, her long muscled legs bore her steadily as she stretched out her calloused hands. "Merciful God! Solomon, Solomon!" The salt tears streamed through the deep lines of her cheeks.

Oh, the joyful, glad reunion of the family! What tears. What rejoicing. What embracing. What warmth of love. What joy of laughter. What blessing of God all about them.

A day before Thanksgiving, Solomon Yoder died. While coughing, his ruptured lungs burst and he drowned in his own blood.

CHAPTER 24

If you were to ask Sarah Yoder how she managed it after Solomon's death, she would have wiped her hands on her apron, brushed back a few wisps of grey hair with worn fingers, and replied, "God's strength. God's strength."

That was almost twenty years ago. My, how things change. Sarah was glad though that there was a little cemetery by the meetinghouse with those deep green cedars scattered here and there over the blowing grass. It didn't look so lonely. Besides, Solomon didn't have to lie without company. Uncle C.P. buried his first wife, Leah, there, a few years back. Now there were about twenty other graves.

Asleep in Jesus. The heart was comforted by an inner knowing that these of their faith, sleeping here, were safe in the arms of Jesus, awaiting the resurrection of the body on that glorious day.

The sacred words of Scripture read by Bishop Jacob Kenagy that day renewed the hope in the hearts of Sarah, Barbara, Salome, and Noah. "But I would not have you ignorant, brethren, concerning them which are asleep, that ye sorrow not, even as others who have no hope. For if we believe that Jesus died and rose again, even so them also which sleep in Jesus will God bring with him."

The church had changed too. Sarah thought it was so much better, people clustering together according to their needs, according to the way they felt the Lord was leading them. They'd outgrown the little Clearfork meetinghouse. Wasn't it a testimony that they, from such varied backgrounds, from so many different states in the union, had solved their problem?

They had differing views on how "plain" was plain for their clothing. Then there was the language. The more progressive ones, who wanted to have a Sunday school right away and who were eager to have English services, built their church three miles down the road, giving it the beautiful name, "Bethel," or "House of God."

Yes, it had worked out fine. One could see the hand of the Lord in it. The Dunkers had moved a couple of miles west and built a little church, Mt. Zion. Then, Sarah and Solomon's group—still used to worshiping in German—had counseled together, prayed, then built their church on that little plot of land by Clearfork Creek, where the huge sycamores blow in the wind. It surely was a beautiful spot.

What a blessing too, that the people kept coming, moving in from Pennsylvania, Ohio, Indiana, Illinois, Michigan, Iowa, Kansas. Why, there must be eight or nine hundred of their people here now, and still they kept coming, moving westward. They hadn't been too uppity selecting a name for their church either. It was a good name, in keeping with plain and simple people—Sycamore Grove. Why not name the church after the handiwork of God, those graceful, white-barked trees, sighing in the wind?

Peaceful. That's what it was. Just plain peaceful. When the double doors in front were opened so a body could look outside and see the flowing grass or the bending trees, or when one could feel the gently flowing, cooling winds, why, it was enough to make a person wonder and worship. It became easy for Sarah to pray, "Lord, thou hast searched and seen me through."

Well, enough of this daydreaming and mind wandering. Sarah had work to be done. It was Thanksgiving Day and she needed to get on with roasting those three fat hens. She was grateful that Salome had split a large supply of wood, stacking it on the back porch.

Barb had made the pies yesterday, four of them: golden-crusted apple, sugar-glazed gooseberry, sitting there giving off a heavenly aroma, sour cherry—red juices bubbling through, and oh yes, don't forget the spicy pumpkin.

How would she have made it without the girls, Salome and Barb? She thought they both were good-looking girls. Better not say pretty, that word wasn't used around here.

Barbara, tall and thin like her mother, swept her black hair back, parted it in the middle, then wrapped it up in a tight bun on the back of her head. Come Sunday, her prayer covering crowned her head, strings flowing down around her shoulders, giving her that finished look a woman of almost thirty-six should have.

Barb Yoder could outwork most women and even some of the men of these parts. Had a good disposition, too. Hummed when she baked or churned. Hardly ever flew off the handle, except that time Old Tillie the cow, who'd bloated herself on spring grass, suddenly threw up her tail during milking.

There was an explosion as Tillie lost control. Barbara was put out, that's for sure. The milk bucket was ruined—Tillie's foot sinking in it that way. Had to pour the milk in the hog trough. Sarah gave thanks that her girls had worked right along with her through the years. Yes. They'd survived.

Salome? Well, one could say she was pretty, fair as she was, and blonde, blue-eyed, that one dimple in her left cheek. But, look out. The menfolk were a little timorous of her fast tongue and step. She hoped Salome would marry someday. Barb too, but, so far they kept their hands to the doughboard or plow handle and their eyes on the stitching and sewing—and the clock, anxious about the time.

"Was it time to bring in the cows? Chickens need feeding? When did we set those hens? Salome, did you try this potato salad recipe?" and on and on. But, that was life—frontier farm life.

Look around. See for yourself. Two cisterns dug and cement-lined. A deep well in the milk house. Smokehouse built. Noah'd put up a summer kitchen so they wouldn't all have to sweat it out in the house during the hot summer. Work, and lots of it. She'd said it was a good verse, "Go to the ant, thou sluggard, consider her ways and be wise."

Guess one could say that the ants would look with favor upon them, Sarah and her three. Not bragging, of course.

She heard the horses neighing as the surrey turned the corner by the barn. Noah and Nettie had arrived. Seven-year-old Seth and his five-year-old brother Simon sat in the back seat.

Nettie, wound up in her brown shawl, head covered with her black Sunday bonnet, held three-year-old Mary Barbara, named after her Aunt Barbara. Nice to keep a name in the family. Guess she'd have to get ready to tell stories. They wanted stories of old times. "How did you and Auntie Barb and Salome an' papa get enough to eat after grandpa died?" And how had they?

If you really want to know, it was that Tozier Hines from the Citizen's Bank over at East Lynne that'd ticked Sarah Yoder off, with him riding up her lane, looking over her fields that way just after Solomon died.

What nerve, let alone the bad manners. She didn't need any dandy in a bowler hat and sharp black suit, to ride by in a new buggy, nodding with that slick smile. No. Sarah knew that Tozier Hines had looked at that note she and Solomon had signed back in 1865. Knew that her payment, plus interest, was coming due in June. She knew also that Tozier had a nice collection of three or four farms around here already, cashing in on the mortgages when the poor, burdened owners couldn't cough up the money.

She decided to show that slick dandy Tozier. Andrew Helmuth, when he found out about old Tozier sizing up her farm that way, said, "Old Tozier's nothin' but a turkey buzzard, circlin' to see what he can get." Well, let him circle. She had news for him.

She got up at four-thirty every morning, except Sundays and those few days when she'd twisted her foot and ankle when it slipped through the flooring of the haymow. Garden work first. Then she'd awaken Noah. He had just turned eleven. Barbara and Salome climbed out of bed then, too. Six o'clock sharp.

The girls headed for the pasture and the milk barn. Noah grabbed a pail for the chicken feed and headed out to the chicken house. Next, he drew water from the cistern north of the house, carried it out to the henhouse, and filled the water pans and troughs. Noah didn't complain. He felt responsible; he did his part.

First chores of the day completed, they gathered around the old oak kitchen table. She had to feed them. They were a hungry brood, growing, working hard. So she shoveled out the brown slices of fried mush and sausage. She passed the homemade blackberry jam as the hot biscuits disappeared into the hungry mouths. She filled milk glasses with last evening's milk, pulled up fresh from the cold well. Couldn't say Sarah Yoder wasn't feeding her brood.

After they'd eaten, Sarah took down the worn Bible that had belonged to Solomon. She kept a little worn paper for a marker to keep her place. It was easy to lose your place in the Bible—and she'd started in Genesis.

Sarah usually read the passage. But after awhile, she let the girls read some of the verses too while she shut her eyes to listen. Noah, the blue-eyed, tanned, barefooted boy, listened attentively to the female voices. When he was bigger, he'd probably have his turn. He was a good and obedient boy, this Noah.

What did it matter who led in the morning devotions? She'd done it all along when Solomon was away in the army. She'd copied down that verse that leveled everything out, like the gospel does, "There is neither Jew nor Greek, male nor female, slave, nor free." That passage always impressed Sarah. She wanted to talk it over sometime with the bishop, Brother Jacob. But, there hadn't been time.

Besides, she was always way over there on the women's side of the church with that partition down the middle. It was hard to get to Brother Jacob. Widow Sarah led her family in morning devotions and she was not ashamed to lift up her voice in prayer. Kneeling too. Right there in the kitchen, all of them turning around, elbows on those cracked and worn bentwood chairs, knees growing callouses on those hard pine floors.

Sarah Yoder's prayers were real as the words poured out from her burdened soul, and out of her great need.

Chapter 25

Salome lifted the green roller blinds at the two dining room windows. Her feet tread softly on the variegated blue rag carpet, stretched and tacked down over straw. She glanced over the table, did she have enough plates?

She didn't take the time to check her hair in the small buffet mirror. Guess they'd have to take her as she was. After all, she was wearing her plum-colored Sunday dress. With her rose and white apron, strings tied in a bow in back, setting off her small waist like that. She guessed she looked more than presentable. Her braided hair, wound around the crown of her head gleamed through her white covering.

"Out o' my way." Barbara bumped her as she hurried out of the kitchen toward the back porch to empty the potato peelings into the slop bucket.

"Now, don't get too excited, Barb. You know what happens when you get on your fast horse." Barbara blushed. Yes, she knew. What Salome referred to was that time last summer when she was selling her produce in East Lynne. Salome had lingered in the store, fingering the fabrics, trying to decide whether or not she could afford the green chambray.

Barb, put out and in a hurry to get home and start canning the sweet corn, had rushed out to the hitching posts. Head down in the wind, she climbed up into the buggy and sat there while the horse dipped his head, reaching for grass by the wooden trough.

But Barb had miscalculated in her hurry. She'd climbed into the wrong buggy. While she was trying to get a small sack of meal, a jug of vinegar and a sack of dried beans to fit into the egg baskets, she was startled by a booming, vibrant male voice.

"Well now, Miss Yoder," said the sun-browned farmer, grinning, eyes twinkling. "I'm a gonna have to take my buggy now."

Mortified wasn't the word for it, as Menno Bender climbed right up and sat down on the buggy seat beside her. She'd had to cover her mouth to hold back the startled cry choking in her throat. Then, out came Salome, getting in on it just as Barbara leaped out of Menno's buggy, which was parked next to hers. It wouldn't have been so bad if Salome hadn't witnessed it.

Salome couldn't keep her mouth shut. She'd tell it at church next Sunday amongst her friends. They'd all roll in laughter, snickering at her dumbness. Oh. For shame! After that, Barb looked several times at the horse and the buggy before she set her foot on the buggy pedal.

Sarah had just come up the basement steps. She grabbed a rag and wiped off a jar of grape juice. The children loved her grape juice. Keep it in the kitchen off of her new rag carpets, that's for sure. Put a lot of labor into those carpets.

"Here comes Uncle C.P and Aunt Mable." Salome hurried to the kitchen window. Frost covered the corners of the glass. They'd brought along old Minnie Hooley from over by the Clearfork Creek bridge. There she hunched, all dressed in her black Sunday dress, huge black bonnet tied under her chin.

Salome resented it a bit, though. Yes, she believed in feeding the widows and the poor, but she knew that after the dinner, old Annie would pull out her clay pipe from her pocket and light up. And, her stories. Why, some of her stories shouldn't be told in front of children, but they crowded at her knee, cheering her on. "Tell more, Annie, tell more!" they'd shout.

They all crowded into the house. You should have heard the merry voices, loud, friendly. Children with lighted faces and rosy cheeks, crying, "Grandma, Grandma. Auntie, Auntie!"

Outside, Samson, the cattle dog, barked, joining in the glee. Samson loved company, too. It meant an extra pan of table scraps for him after the dinner.

How Uncle C. P.'s oldest, Dave, had matured now. His eyes glistened along with his shiny black hair. White teeth gleamed from his smiling lips. His coloring was like Barb's. He'd married Susan Harder, and she was as fair as Salome. Ten-year-old Allen, their oldest, would soon be prodding Sarah Yoder to let loose with her stories on how she survived when Grandpa Solomon died. Then, if there was time enough, handsome, dark-skinned Dave would lead them in some hymns.

Sarah's heart warmed and mellowed. She rejoiced and gave thanks for such blessings—a roof over her head, this farm, all this marvelous food. Yes, it was grace, the grace of God. God had given her brokenness and sorrow, seedtime and harvest. She'd drunk from the cup of bereavement and sadness, and from the horn of plenty. She'd discovered that, indeed, this was life—the Lord giving and taking away.

Sarah's gentle smile lighted her face. Her dark eyes gleamed beneath her lined brow. Her silver hair, parted in the middle, matched her prayer covering with the strings tied under her chin. Oh, joyful day—family, singing, eating, giving thanks. What would she do without church and family, the Bible, the songs, the gently murmured prayers of her people? They sometimes argued too much over small details, but they were good people—the kind of people one could call one's own, the kind of people spoken of in the Scriptures as "brethren and sisters in the Lord."

Noah's prayer set the mood of thankfulness, joy, and praise. Fourteen of them sat around the table. What dishes! Barb's homemade bread was making the bend at the end of the table, while Aunt Mable's smoked ham followed after. Sarah's baked hens, slices piled high, came next.

It took a while to get mashed potatoes and the right amount of gravy on the children's plates. Old Annie Hooley put both elbows on the table and held her fork like she was going to stab an air pocket in a gooseberry pie. She dipped her head near her plate and began to shovel.

Sarah tried not to mind the beet juice that got spilled on her best tablecloth. Let Salome worry about that; Salome was the best at getting rid of stains. Before they served the pie, she guessed she'd better let loose with those stories. Otherwise, the children would never give her any peace.

"How did we make it when Grandpa Solomon died? Well, I've already told you that we worked. Got up early. Oh, yes, I almost forgot, we picked gooseberries."

And, they had. They picked until their fingers bled. Sarah'd taken the note to the bank soon after Solomon died to find out from Mr. Tozier just how much she would need to pay. She left the children sitting outside in the buggy. They'd sat, solemn, unsmiling, worried about their mother in that brick building, sitting in front of that strange man.

"Why, Mrs. Yoder," Tozier cleared his throat and took off his wire-framed glasses. "We're going to have to have all of it. Let's see, on your note, that would be one hundred and fifty dollars."

Sarah remembered that she had almost fainted. Catching herself, she sat up straight and looked Tozier Hines straight in the face. "We've all been half ruined by the grasshoppers. You know that, Mr. Tozier. Give me some time. I know with next year's crop I can pay two hundred next year."

"Gotta have the interest plus the payment. Too bad about the grasshoppers. Did your late crop come in at all, Mrs. Yoder?" he said, thinking of the three farms he'd foreclosed on last month.

"Well, I didn't get anywhere with Tozier. I put the children, that's your aunts, Barb and Salome, and your father,

Noah, in the back of the buggy so's they couldn't see my face while I drove old Dink home. But they knew I was crying, anyway."

Sarah remembered how sick it had made her. She couldn't eat for three days. She wandered over the farm, giving her mind and spirit time and room to search for answers. Just when she thought she'd have to head for Bishop Kenagy's or over to Uncle C.P.'s and ask for a handout, Noah and Salome came running out of the woods.

"Mother! The gooseberries, the gooseberries, and they're sour, mother, green and sour."

"Why do they call them gooseberries if there aren't any geese?" asked little Simon, waving his fork.

"Don't know the answer to that, Simon, but you ought to ask your father and Aunt Salome and Aunt Barb about how we picked gooseberries."

Surely they'd stripped every single gooseberry bush in those acres of woods. And the chiggers! Don't even think of it. Sweat, heat, flies, tall grass. Oh, the snakes, big ones, bull snakes and black snakes, and Barbara always expected to come across a timber rattler. "Have you ever picked a gooseberry?" Sarah looked over at her grandsons. "You couldn't begin to count the scratches on our hands and arms from the thorns.

"How much did you get for them?" queried Seth.

"We sold them at five cents a gallon. Five cents a gallon." If you listened closely, you could hear the drop and the break in Sarah's voice, and the fleeting look of pain that crossed her brow, opened up again like this to the hardships of earlier days.

"In heat and in rain we picked gooseberries. Gallons and gallons of gooseberries. Guess it was kinda' a blessing from God, like the manna in the wilderness spread everywhere. I don't know if I ever saw so many big green gooseberries as what grew that year."

Barbara and Salome had gotten tired and wanted to quit. "Let old man Tozier have the land," they said. "But your father stood in front of the girls and said, 'Well, Barb and Salome, if Tozier gets the land where are you gonna sleep?' That did it. Those girls were back in the woods with their buckets soon after sunup.

"We sold about five hundred gallons at five cents a gallon. Let's see," Sarah pondered a moment. "That'd be twenty-five dollars, wouldn't it? Yes, twenty-five dollars. The four of us worked in the heat all through June, neglecting the garden, picking those berries."

"Who bought 'em, Grandma?" the children wanted to know.

"Folks at church. Thank goodness Mennonite folk like gooseberry pie. Then I sold some at the grocery stores. Folks called me the gooseberry lady. Guess I felt a little queer and odd, but we saved the farm."

Sarah did like the widow in the Bible who finally got what she needed by going and asking, over and over again. "I made four more trips to that bank." Sarah took a couple of sips from her coffee cup. "Better get started on these pies. Who wants gooseberry?" She chuckled.

"I do, I do," shouted the children.

"The gooseberries weren't enough. I had to add on what Barbara earned from her week over at Hostetlers after Bertha had those twins. We ate beans and cornmeal and what we could from the garden. Sold the cream and eggs. I took in seventy-three dollars to that slick Tozier fellow. I looked directly at him, handed him the money, and said I'd bring in the rest come fall after we'd picked, shelled, and sold the walnuts and the hickory nuts. Surprised, too, he was. Hadn't expected me to have such a large payment. Well, that left seventy-seven dollars. Noah, tell the children about the walnuts."

Noah, white teeth grinning through his red lips, brushed back his hair after he'd taken a bite from his cherry pie. "Can't say I know anything gets the hands blacker than hulling black walnuts. No sir. Can't begin to get it off. Barbara and Salome had stained hands, too. Had to go to school like that. Everybody laughed at us and called us the two-toned Yoders. That's right. After a couple of days, we laughed, too. Must of hulled 200 bushels of walnuts that fall. After that, the hickory nuts were nothing. Sweep 'em up off the ground. Most of the shells fell off anyway. Big ones, small ones, all sizes. Salome and Grandma sorted them according to the sizes. Guess we musta' had nigh on to couple hundred bushels of hickory nuts."

"How'd you sell them?" Simon asked, shoveling in his pie.

"Well, ask your Aunt Salome that. She'll tell you."

"We hitched up the spring wagon, put on our wraps, and headed for Garden City. Yep. That's what your pa and me did. Sat there in front of Kimberling's store peddling nuts to folks passing by. Embarrassed? Well, I probably was. But your pa had a good time. Met some fine folks. Looking back, I reckon it was good for me. Anyway, no one ever called me the 'nut lady.'" She roared amidst the hoots of laughter. "Yes, Mama saved the farm with our help."

Seth had finished his cherry pie and allowed as how he wanted to try the gooseberry. His Aunt Barb slipped a sugary piece on his plate. "Tell me a story, Aunt Barb."

Right then the only story Aunt Barb could tell was the one about the bishop trickin' those easterners who wanted to move in here with their strict rules and regulations about clothes. Barb began telling about Bishop Kenagy who'd received a letter from that Amish Mennonite group from back in Ohio. How they would like to come on the train out here to Cass County, Missouri, and size up the land.

They also allowed as they were extra plain in their dress. Wouldn't this community appreciate that? Well, Bishop Kenagy had got a lot of those questions about whether or not hooks and eyes or buttons were the right thing for Christians answered already.

That had been the first Amish Mennonite conference held here at Sycamore Grove. Folks came here from all over. Got that one settled too. Buttons passed. Folks could sew buttons on their clothes if they wanted to. Sure, some of the plainer ones continued to wear hooks and eyes. Then, these men were pushing the beard for all men of the church, too.

Well, Bishop Kenagy didn't want such strictness introduced again in his church. He met these gentlemen, six or seven of them, at the depot in Harrisonville, and brought them out to size up the land. Only thing though, Bishop Kenagy dressed up for the occasion. Yes. Found that stiff boiled shirt of his oldest boy, Steven. Put it on with its standup collar, donned a tie, then borrowed Steven's bowler hat. Yep. Rode out to meet these plain types all dressed up like a dandy.

All day they looked at land. Bishop Kenagy even took them to the hotel for lunch at noon. Everybody ate their lunch and talked about the land. No one mentioned hooks and eyes, or how long a beard should be, or what kind of bonnets the women should wear. Nothing.

Bishop Kenagy waved them a good-bye, his bowler hat in his hand, outstretched and waving in the wind. "Brethren never once mentioned dress or their rules and regulations," said Bishop Kenagy. And, that was the last anyone around here ever saw or heard from them.

There were murmurs and chuckles at the wisdom and trickery of their bishop. Actually, everyone was a bit surprised, but if you knew Bishop Kenagy, you would understand and forgive him.

"Well, about time to rid up this table and get started with the dishes. Grandchildren, you all gonna help me?" teased Sarah, looking out of the northeast window to the tall oak and hickory woods beyond, all yellow and scarlet in their flaming colors.

She and her children had saved the land. It was good land. Land for sowing and pastureland. Trees. Timber and berries, flowing creeks lined with hazelnut and blackberries. Good land. Next year, maybe they could start enlarging the house. Yes, if the family kept on growing they'd need more room.

But before they'd left the table, old Annie Hooley let loose with one of her remarks. You know. I warned you. A slip of grease ran down her chin while cherry juice from her pie stained the corner of her mouth. She waved her fork and cackled, "Too bad this here chair I'm a sittin' in ain't got a hole in the bottom, so's I could jes' keep on eatin'!"

Chapter 26

It was a blessing, living in a Christian community like this. Noah Yoder was going over it in his mind on the journey homeward from Sunday services. He felt renewed; his heart gladdened. He pulled the reins, guiding Sol and Gent around a huge chunk of mud that'd fallen from a wagon wheel last week. "Bust a buggy wheel on that," he said to himself.

In the back seat, Nettie hummed, soft and low. She held Mary Barbara on her lap. This April day suited her just fine. How mellow. How good the sunshine, warming her right side as they rocked homeward. Little Mary Barbara began singing with her, "The way of the cross leads home, the way of the cross leads home."

Seth and Simon sat beside her on her left. Good boys, they were, faces quiet, eager to arrive home and sit at her table. They'd have fried chicken today. She'd mash the potatoes and make gravy. Menfolk liked it that way, didn't they?

Then she noticed. Why was Seth up there with his father so quiet? Seth Yoder was quiet because he was in pain. He was in pain because he had cut his finger. His left hand was hidden in his coat pocket, and if you looked closely, you could see the white corner of his handkerchief sticking out of the edge of the pocket. The handkerchief was tightly wrapped around the bleeding finger.

But what made it even worse, and why Seth kind of

hung his head like he did, was that he had cut his finger that morning in service. Yes, in church, and even worse, during prayer. Guilt swelled up in the young lad, souring his stomach. Sooner or later one of them would notice his finger. After all, a fourteen-year-old boy can't keep his finger hidden in his pocket all day, wrapped in his white handkerchief.

And that was another matter. Mother didn't like blood on white handkerchiefs; it gave her a pain getting the stain removed. One trouble piled up upon another.

And the throb! The awful throbbing of his hand. The cut was clean, right to the bone on his finger next to the thumb. He'd remembered to shut his knife and slip it back into his pocket. Tillman Yost, kneeling in prayer beside him had his eyes open and gasped a little when he saw Seth's knife slip as he was trying to carve his name in the oaken bench.

Ought not to try to carve your name in oak. Any fool ought to know it'd take practically a lifetime, hard as that oak wood is. Seth blamed the preacher though, standing up there preaching in a language that he didn't understand.

German preaching. That's the way preaching was here at Sycamore Grove. Older folks understood Preacher Hartzler real well. Take his class, those seventeen boys all lined up on those two front benches, sweating it out, twisting; fathers over on the left on those side benches looking straight at them, stern as that stone face he'd had to read about in his reader, what was it called? "The Great Stone Face."

Serious stuff here at church. Seth liked singing, and they were singing in English now. Not all of the preachers preached in German now either. It was just Brother Hartzler's turn and he couldn't quite hack that English grammar. Slowed him down so much, he figured that it was the congregation's duty to keep up with him. German was a good language, wasn't it? Helped keep them separate. God's people—their clothing, their language, their ways, their food.

The Mennonite way. He knew that much, Seth did. But

most of the boys were turned off by that preacher's hour-and-a-half sermons. Sometimes they were even two hours long.

When they had finally knelt for closing prayer—turned around, elbows on the bench—the closing prayer went on and on, too. Everyone's knees ached. People adjusted their backs and legs several times, as reverently as possible, trying to keep their kneecaps from bearing down on a crack between the floorboards.

That's when the knives had come out. First it'd been Amos Troyer, shoving back his shock of hair, grinning, digging on the "o" in his name. He'd been working on it for the past three services. Then Howard Erb followed, sticking out his tongue as he dug, starting on his last name. If you ever saw the bench, you'd know that there were others besides these three—the telltale marks were there.

The buggy passed the big Osage orange tree by the barnyard. Home now. What would Seth do? He'd have to change clothes, then run out there and open that gate to let the sheep out of the barnyard. Father expected that. Had to go to the privy, too. Couldn't keep his throbbing finger in his pocket forever. What had they learned when they were little tykes in Sister Hallman's class? "Be sure your sins will find you out," wasn't it?

He'd decided to go to his mother about it first. Getting past her first reaction, she would make it easier to pass the information on to Father. Before he could do it though, he was betrayed by his sister, Mary Barbara. The bright little child, pigtails swinging over her pinafore in the back, caught sight of the tightly-wrapped finger, blood staining the handkerchief. "Seth cut his finger. Seth cut his finger!" she called, pointing to the blood-soaked handkerchief.

Nettie placed the cast-iron skillet filled with the cut-up pieces of the young fryer on the Home Comfort range. She turned. Concern spread across her face as she took four steps across the kitchen to her son. Well, he'd had it now. "How'd this happen? Seth, what happened?" Her flour-coated fingertips clasped the throbbing hand, unbinding it. "Oh, Seth, what a gash. Tell me what happened."

Like all boys caught in a dilemma, few words as possible are best.

"Cut it."

"Cut it? Yes, Seth, I see you cut it. But what happened? Just how did you cut it?" Pain swept across her brow as she felt the throb of Seth's finger.

"Just cut it." Oh, mercy, if Seth could only hide. Next, Father would be in on this.

"Let us see, let us see!" Simon and Mary Barb cried together, grabbing at the wounded finger.

"Children, get back. Father, come here. Seth's cut his finger clean to the bone." She pushed her adolescent son into a kitchen chair, as the blood had drained from his face.

Well, Father did come. And they found out, all of them, about how Seth Yoder cut his finger.

Seth's father knew, even as the words spilled out of his mouth. "Son, how did you do this?" He'd been a boy once too. Maybe the services had been even longer in his day. He remembered the gouges on church benches in his time.

Seth had to sit there and spill out the whole sorry story while his father got the enamel basin, soap, and water, and began to gently wash the offending member with his giant farmer's hands.

Tenderly, lovingly, Noah washed his son's shameful finger. Nettie would have done it, but Noah volunteered. This allowed Nettie to get back to the fried chicken and the potatoes that would soon need to be mashed.

Applying the Mercurochrome, he blew on it a bit, then wrapped Seth's finger in a narrow band from that torn white cloth Nettie'd provided. "Were you carving in church? On the church bench?"

Father's questions got the story out. Fact was, Seth actually felt less guilty getting it out. But would he be forgiven? He felt so shameful. What to do?

"Let's go open the gate together." Noah Yoder placed his arm around his sheepish adolescent son's shoulders. Seth rose. They walked together. Better, getting it all out like this.

"Father, I can't understand what Preacher Hartzler's sayin', most of us boys don't know. Do you understand him, Father?"

"Well, yes, son. I understand Brother Hartzler's sermons. Guess it's kind of hard for you youngsters since we don't speak High German at home. Does leave you youngsters kind of stranded, doesn't it?"

Chapter 27

No, Noah didn't use the rod on his son, Seth. Didn't believe in whipping children, let alone using a stick or paddle. He and Nettie believed their yes, their no, and the limits they enforced were "the shaping rod." The times when words were spoken firmly, looks too—all of it.

He remembered how his father told of the merciless beatings in army prisons. No. Confession and restitution are what's needed when we sin. Restitution. That's what Seth agreed upon that day with his father.

Seth had broken down and cried at Preacher Hartzler's house. Amos Troyer and Howard Erb were there too with their fathers who stood there before Preacher Hartzler. The teenagers hung their heads.

Sobs shook Seth as he caught his breath and pushed out the words. "I'm sorry, Preacher Hartzler. I don't want to desecrate the house of God. Forgive me, I'm sorry."

Howard and Amos cried too. All of them were now on their way to East Lynne to get putty, sandpaper, and paint to fix the bench. "Would Brother Hartzler have a key to the meetinghouse?"

Then Amos Troyer blurted out, "Preacher Hartzler, we can't understand you, speakin' them long sermons like you do in German. Folks talk Pennsylvania Dutch around home, then they talk in English. I can understand the Pennsylvania Dutch, but your German sounds like Greek to me."

Now what? Would this noble preacher, bishop to boot, be put off and offended? But Preacher Hartzler said: "Sit down, boys. I want you to try. You know we have two years of German taught over there at Clearfork school. Lots of our folk speak German. It sharpens the mind to learn it. Language of the Bible." He meant, of course, that big leather bound Martin Luther Bible he read from up there from behind that handhewn pulpit.

"The marks of nonconformity to the world, our plain dress, the German language, language of prayer and the Bible, especially for worship. You are all forgiven. You must repair the bench—and use your own money doing it. The sacrifice will help you remember."

There went Seth Yoder's money for that baseball bat he'd seen in the store window. But there were problems over that too—playing ball. Some things about being a Christian in this community confused him. Anyway, Bishop Hartzler was kind and good. They were forgiven, that's what counted.

Maybe he'd earn enough money to buy the bat later. But as for now, there went the thirty-six cents he'd been saving for three months. All spent on his folly and foolishness. Then Seth remembered his father's piercing question, "How'll you feel, Seth, when you have your own children and bring them to services and you slide in on that bench, your carved initials grinning there before your innocent children?" Well, that remark was a clincher, for certain. It made sense and hit home.

Seth hoped in vain that Grandma Sarah Yoder and his Aunt Barb and Aunt Salome hadn't found out about his indiscretion. News about what happened to Seth and his friends spread faster than crabgrass after a summer rain. Cough at one edge of the Mennonite community and by evening it's heard at the farthest edge on the other side. That's right. But, it's mostly because of the caring; people do care for one another. After they finish talking about it, getting the words out, sharing it, mulling over it, then they do like St. Paul in the Bible, gird their loins and do something about it. Sarah Yoder did.

Sarah insisted that Salome stay home—quilt, go pick berries in the woods, hoe the garden, anything. Sarah had a need to hook up the horse to the buggy and take the eggs and cream over to East Lynne herself.

Hadn't she had enough practice after all these years? It was good for an old lady to take an airing; to get out, to get away from the limits of her farm. Ride through the fresh air. See who painted his barn. Check how the crops were growing in the neighbor's fields. She'd insisted so strongly that both Barb and Salome let her do it.

They didn't like it that she stayed so long, though. They worried about her. She was getting on in years, and though she didn't complain, they knew she had a dizzy spell once in awhile when the temperature rose up around ninety-five.

Coming back from the produce store in East Lynne, egg and cream money in her purse, she turned in to Bishop Hartzler's driveway. Nice place. Sturdy barn. Good shingle roof. Fine coat of paint. Tall trees. Thank God, these folks had foresight to plant maple, oak, and ash trees.

The house too rose up plain, stark, two-storied. Solid, like the house of a bishop ought to be. She hoped Bishop Hartzler wasn't out in the field, but if he was she was prepared to straddle a fence wire and sally out to see him. Sarah Yoder had something she wanted to discuss with her bishop.

Ruth, his kindly wife, told Sarah that, yes, the bishop was out in the field. Plowing, as a matter of fact. Sister Hartzler smiled broadly, proudly: "Plowing with our new sulky plow."

Sarah herself had been wanting to get one of those new-fangled sulky plows. She wouldn't mind riding to and fro across the field, furrows splitting beneath her as she laid open the east twenty acres. She better go ahead and jar loose and get a sulky plow. If the bishop set the pattern, it was all right for the rest to follow, wasn't it?

Sister Hartzler wanted her to sit and pass the hour with her, but Sarah persevered. Following Sister Hartzler's pointing finger, she headed toward the southwest corner of the field.

Yes, she could see the bishop plowing there. "Good time to be preparing next week's sermon," thought Sarah. Not at all like the plowing she'd done, holding the plow down into that sod, heaving her body, calling out to the horses, slapping the reins. Real work, that was. Looked like fun, this sulky plow, rolling back and forth across the land. Why, yes, Brother Hartzler could indeed think about next week's sermon with such effortless work, and think about it in English!

Riding that sulky plow was more fun, especially with this matched team, thought Bishop Hartzler, as the shiny steel wheels of his plow rolled along over the even field, black earth spreading beneath him. He was thinking of his next sermon on 2 Timothy 1:7: "For God hath not given us the spirit of fear; but of power, and of love, and of a sound mind."

What a wonderful verse God had given him. He let the words flood his mind again in the language of his preaching, German. Then he noticed a tall woman striding briskly down the pasture toward the corner where he would soon turn around with his team and new plow.

Why, if it didn't look like Sarah Yoder. What would be so important that a woman of his church would take it upon herself to climb through the barbed-wire fence to meet him in the field? A death? Bad news? Why hadn't Ruth just rung the dinner bell there by the porch? He and the team would have headed there immediately.

"Whoa!" Bishop Hartzler held the reins back firmly, stopping his team under the shade of a hackberry tree. The bishop, remembering his manners, tipped his straw hat as he turned his bearded, tanned face toward Sarah. "Afternoon, Sarah. Surprised me. Didn't expect a woman comin' out to my field this afternoon." He waited, a little solemn. Surely, Sarah's news must be something tragic.

"Afternoon, Bishop Hartzler, afternoon." The wind whipped her calico dress around her tall form. Her brown hand drew back the brim of her sunbonnet. She wanted an audience with the bishop, face-to-face. She wanted to see him, and she wanted him to see and listen to her and not miss a word. She'd thought about it a lot—no use hesitating about it any longer.

"Brother Hartzler." Her voice was strong, even though her heart was beating rapidly. She caught her breath just as she was going to ask him to get off his plow and step over to the shade under the tree. But, Bishop Hartzler had already tied his reins and was sliding off the plow seat to join her under the hackberry.

"Somethin' I just have to talk to you about. I tried to bring up my children in the Lord. We lived through war and hard times. Still, Solomon and I longed for a church. When we could, we took our children to services, even in the worst weather. For years, I, a widow woman, took it on my own shoulders. Church is important in my family."

Now just what was this elderly sister of his congregation getting at? And, my, wasn't she coming at it with fervor? Make a good preacher herself. Expresses herself right well, thought Bishop Hartzler, wiping the sweat from his pink brow. Sarah continued.

"Last week my grandson, Seth Yoder, was here at your place. We all know what he and some others his age did in church. We all know too that it was wrong. Now, I understand the boys all came over here and asked you to forgive them. Them boys made it right. Bought supplies out of their own pockets and fixed the bench just as good as new. I went to the meetinghouse and took a look myself. Brother Hartzler, no offense, but how can you justify preaching in a language these youngsters don't understand, hour-and-a-half sermons and long prayers to boot?"

Well, Sarah'd got the words out, and again, her body and spirit stayed together. Just now she noticed how weak her legs felt, but her long skirt and the blowing wind covered their trembling.

She'd been bold. But hadn't those other women been bold? Miriam taking the lead, dancing and singing like she did? Ruth in Boaz's field, lying at the foot of his blanket at night? Jael? Well, better leave her out—driving a tent stake through an evil man's head was too much. There were better ways of bringing justice than that. She could name many other women who took the lead.

Then Sarah's spirit faltered a little, as a faintness and doubt spread over her. Maybe she'd overstepped her bounds, coming out here like this. Maybe this was work for the deacon. As her self-doubt grew, the trembling in her legs increased. Her left hand touched her chin, an automatic response to the slight tremor she felt there.

"Why, no. Why, Sarah." Bishop Hartzler was a bit taken. Jarred. A part of him trembled—only inside—like something pecking away at an important edge of his being, of who he was. Kind of like a woodpecker pecking a hole in a trunk of a tree.

"Ahem! Well, now, Sarah, uh, uh, why, how you surprise me. Can't remember any folks in our congregation, no adults, members of the church, bringing that up to me like you just did. Ahem." He looked at Sarah, solemnly, then wiped his brow again. "Like I told the boys, we are nonconformed people. We have our marks that show us different from the world. You know what they are, Sarah. Terrible thing when a church loses its marks of distinction and merges with the world. None of us want that. Why, your covering, you sisters with your plain dresses and bonnets, the men with plain suits and no ties, the beards that God gave us—all mark us off from the world. Then our doctrines, what we believe about turning the other cheek..."

Sarah interrupted. "I know all that, Bishop Hartzler. I'm not here to tear anything down, just to help build up. Have you ever been in a crowd of people where you could not understand a word? Not a single word? Don't you think that is what Seth was trying to tell you? You know the church changes, ways change, clothes change."

Sarah was certain even that the Bible itself was written in other languages first, what was it, Hebrew, Greek? She could have spoken longer on this, but she realized she was running the risk of getting long-winded.

Sarah'd scored a point here. Bishop Hartzler had been in that Swedish Lutheran community out in Kansas once, and as far as he was concerned, he'd might just as well been trying to understand the cackling of a bunch of prairie hens. He couldn't understand a word.

"Well, our youth are the future of the church. And, look at our country. English is the language. How many youngsters of our church actually enroll in those German lessons over at Clearfork?"

Sarah'd scored a point there, too. Some lived so far away that they simply couldn't make it and do the needed farm work. Others simply didn't care, didn't have interest. They went to a school where lessons were taught in English. What do you need two languages for anyway, out here in Missouri?

Bishop Hartzler felt the stress. It pressed down on him. Give him time to work it out. Besides, didn't they know how he faltered, hesitated, searched for the right word when he had to run a sentence through his head and translate it into English? "Others feel this way too, Sarah?" He looked tired, worried.

"It's more than one would like to think, Brother Hartzler. Give it some thought. Give it some thought." She felt sorry for him. She knew he cared deeply about their souls. He was a loving and gentle man. He stumbled and tottered around like a duck trying to hurry to the pond when he spoke at any length in English. Maybe she'd truly overstepped her bounds, forgetting that—according to St. Paul—Christians are to be obedient to those who have charge over their souls. What now?

Sarah allowed as how she had to get on home. Salome and Barb would be worried about her. Besides, they had all that garden stuff stacked up to peel, shell, and can, let alone do the evening chores.

She bade the gentle bishop good-bye and turned toward the barn and her waiting horse and buggy. A slight depression swept down on her. She asked herself, "Did I make a mistake?" Nothing had changed. The doubt grew. "What have I done?" she thought. "Overstepped my bounds, that's what. Old woman like me climbing these fences to confront the bishop about his preaching."

Who'd she think she was anyway? She remembered. She'd overstepped her bounds once before, long ago, by taking on baking bread at that hotel up in Harrisonville. Shame engulfed her as she remembered her sorry dough climbing up that mill wheel paddle like it did. Who knew what would climb up over this visit to the bishop.

Chapter 28

The meetinghouse was filled that Sunday morning in May. The double doors on each side of the sanctuary were opened wide. In silence they sat, sober, plainly garbed. Row on row of white-covered women. Row on row of solemn, dark-clothed farm men waiting like Trappist monks, silent before their bowl and bread.

Soon the bishop would stand behind the pulpit and bring the word. The plainness of the meetinghouse—its starkness, the solemnity of the worshipers—was in stark contrast with nature's flamboyant burst outside those double doors.

Billows of white clouds swept over the blue sky. Tall, white-barked sycamores shook in the wind, flashing the yellow green of their spring growth. Heady fragrance drifted upward towards the open doors from the waxy May apples clustering in the shade of the elms by the fence. Brother Helmuth tapped his tuning fork against his hymnal. He hummed two notes, sounding the pitch, then he lifted his left arm and began the hymn:

> Be silent, be silent, A whisper is heard,
> Be silent, and listen, Oh treasure each word.
>
> Be silent, be silent, For holy this place,
> This altar that echoes The message of grace.

Tread softly, tread softly, The Master is here;
Tread softly, tread softly, He bids us draw near.

Even the boys who had carved their initials irreverently only days earlier held their hymnals, heads lifted, eyes glistening, as the balm of that sacred chorus bathed their souls. The song rose up gently and full, then dropped, guided by Brother Helmuth's hand. They waited. The Master was there.

Then came the sermon. Bishop Hartzler wore his best black suit that day. His grey hair, combed and parted on the side, and his grey-white beard gave him the air of a patriarch as he rose sturdily before them.

Liebe Brueder und Schwestern! "Dear Brothers and Sisters!" German. German again? Sarah Yoder's starched grey dress crinkled as she leaned forward to look between Orpha Zook and Matilda Hershberger's shoulders.

Never had Sarah Yoder, Noah Yoder and his family, and especially Seth Yoder, with his still bandaged finger, ever heard such precise, clear, clipped, and expressive German as fell from Bishop Hartzler's lips that morning.

The Lord had given him his text that day on the plow: *Gott hat uns nicht die faehigkeit angst zu haben gegeben sondern kraft zu haben.* "For God hath not given us the spirit of fear, but of power...."

Clearing his throat when he'd finished the verse, he looked both ways, surveying the innocent eyes of the dear sisters, the forthrightness and earnestness of the brethren on the right. Ah, a good day for the power of the Lord through his word.

Er hat uns das Wort gegeben. "He has given us the Word."

With fortitude and power, Bishop Hartzler preached. The words spilled out in front of the hand-hewn pulpit like golden corn spilling out of a hand-cranked corn sheller. Strong words. Sturdy words. Words to live by.

Wir sind aussergewoehnliche Menschen. "We are a people set apart."

Wir sind befohlen, ein heiliges und einfaches leben zu fuehren. "We are called to keep his holy and simple ways."

Wir sind das Licht der Welt. "We are the light to the world."

He went on and on. No inner doubt crept up on the bishop's face. Surety. Strength. Never was Bishop Hartzler's German so perfectly spoken. The guttural sounds ripped and tore through the meetinghouse. An infant, awakening to such fervor, whimpered and began to cry. Seth Yoder and Amos Troyer, sitting under their fathers' watchful eyes, looked up, wide-eyed in awe, even if they understood not a word.

Their hearts pounded. They could not even relieve the tension building up by fingering the pearl handles of their pocket knives, as their fathers had confiscated them this Lord's day. The freshly repaired bench would stay repaired.

It was an hour of contrast. Sarah and Barb Yoder over left on the women's side battled within over how to await the word from the Master this hour, all the while the rising taste of resentment was seeping on the edges of their tongues.

"Well," thought Sarah. "This is what I get for being so forward."

They tried to subdue the flesh, its assertions and kickbacks. Patience, endurance. That's what they all would learn, plus getting Seth Yoder in those German classes over at that Clearfork school. If her religion required sermons in German, Sarah Yoder vowed her family wouldn't disgrace the church.

Seth Yoder was a bright lad. Given time, she could teach him herself. No, we have to knuckle under again.

Noah and Nettie twisted too. Discipline is needed to be a faithful servant of Christ. Maybe the heart heard the words better, understood them better in German. Noah listened carefully too, but if you looked closely you could note a tinge of sadness mixed with the pride and admiration he felt for that handsome lad, his son over there on that center bench near the front. His mind drifted. Could he spare Seth a few weeks and hours to get him over to that school and learn German?

Then the bishop who'd soared mightily in that high-ceilinged meetinghouse that hour, began to descend. More lowly, more softly, came his words. Even words of care and love. Why, here he was, calling on them to sing that old German hymn, "Gott Ist Die Liebe."

Gott ist die Liebe, Laesst mich erloesen. Gott ist die Liebe, er liebt auch mich. Drum sag ich's noch einmal. Gott ist die liebe, er liebt auch mich. "God is love, He saved me. God is love, He also loved me. That's why I say it again, God is love, and He also loves me."

What a soft ending for a sermon of power. How the words mellowed when sung in perfect four-part harmony. As the sisters' sweet voices rose, the men's strong bass and tenor gave foundation. The sound mingled with the sweet sights, sounds, and smells of springtime flowing in through the open doors. If you looked closely, even the Sweet William blooming by the sidewalk swayed in the wind, keeping the rhythm of the gentle hymn, calling them to love and peaceful living under the gracious love of God. And, in German, too.

That night, Bishop Hartzler tossed and turned in his sleep. Great heaviness swept over him. Something pulled and drew at his feet like black floodwaters. Part of his soul was aware that another part of his soul was troubled. He was weeping. Salt tears, hot and heavy, spilled down upon his pillowcase. Then the symbol cleared through the fog of his semiconscious mind. What symbol? Water, life-giving water, cool and clear, flowing from a pump.

There he stood—a bishop—on a green hillside, and the congregation gathered all around, Seth Yoder and Amos Troyer were standing there in front. More tears fell. For these gathered here were surely not of his congregation, were they?

So beggarly they were. Tired, needy, clothes tattered.

How weary and poor they looked. The hot sun bore down upon them as they stretched out their arms, their hands holding cups. Parched, desert dry, their throats were. And he, the bishop, stood on his hill under a shade tree, looking down. He pumped faster, muscles in his arm aching. His other hand beckoned to the tattered, parched crowd. He lifted his voice and pleaded, *Komm und trink! Komm und trink!* "Come and drink! Come and drink!"

No one came. They turned to one another. All had bewildered, confused, and worried looks on their faces. Then, they crowded closer to the pump. How foolish. Yet, they did not fill their cups and drink.

KOMM UND TRINK! He shouted, exasperated. Surely, he thought, his congregation were not such foolish sheep. The sheep know the shepherd's voice, don't they?

By this time, his tossings, mumblings, and turnings had awakened Ruth. She rose up in fright, shaking him forcefully. "John! John!" Grabbing his shoulder, she shook him. "John, wake up, you're dreaming!"

Bishop Hartzler arose and wandered about the house in his nightdress. His feverish mind tried to attach a meaning to his dream. Could it be? Could it be that the dear brethren and sisters, but even more importantly, the blessed young people, could not drink? That they had parched spirits because they could not understand him? He shook his head, held his jaw in his hands, and bowed in sadness.

The worst part of the dream had been when that old frontier woman who'd suffered so in the Civil War, Sarah Yoder, in a faded sunbonnet and tattered dress, barefooted, pushed her way through the gathered congregation under that blazing sun.

She'd marched right up to the mound and planted her soiled feet on that rich green grass. She'd shoved him aside, grabbed the pump handle as she said, "We have to water the flock, Brother Hartzler. Come and drink." In English, too. She beckoned to the thirsty ones below. "Come and drink!"

As he had looked out over the beggarly-looking people circled around him, a tender looking lad with liquid pools for eyes kept lifting up his hand to show him a lacerated, bleeding finger. Three times, the lad had come through the crowd to show him his terrible wound.

Sarah Yoder's words chilled him, called out that way in English, "Come and drink."

Next Sunday service, Bishop Hartzler, a gentle modesty in his step, rose to his pulpit, cleared his throat, and told the assembled worshipers his revealing dream. "I shall no longer preach in German," he said tenderly, and a bit sadly, in faltering English.

Chapter 29

Sarah and Salome Yoder sat on the long, wide north porch of the remodeled farmhouse. My, how nice it was, sitting here in the shade, a gentle breeze touching their cheeks. Their hands were busy peeling tomatoes from the garden.

Here it was July 10, and already they had all these tomatoes to can. Sarah's hair, snow white, softened the lines in her face. Still, her eyes were dark, her vision sharp. Age had not slowed down her nimble fingers.

"Put some more tomatoes in my pail," she called to Salome, who'd gotten up to stretch herself a bit.

"Don't rightly know if we should have spent the money, but isn't it a blessing, all the room we have?"

"Mother, we needed the room. Crops have been good. Don't you remember what President McKinley said in his campaign last year, 'A full dinner pail in every man's hand.' Besides, lots of folks in this community have built new houses. Why, I'd call some of them just plain prestigious. That's what, prestigious. Let alone the way folks have been measuring their barns and outbuildings, giving the dimensions to that new writer. What's his name, Glenn?

"Well, what do you think the bishop will say when he sees the book that Glenn put out? We don't intend to have our farm in that book at all. Pride. That's what it looks like to me." Salome focused her blue eyes beyond the barn to the fat milk cows grazing in the north pasture.

There just may have been some real, living pride in the hearts of those Mennonite farmers who were interviewed by Mr. Glenn for his history book of Cass County.

Hadn't they worked for what they had? And Mr. Glenn had acknowledged their religion. When the book came out, the sentences seemed to read kindly and warmheartedly: "Mr. Miller is a member of the religious society of the Mennonites and is highly respected by all who know him as a conscientious and consistent member. By occupation he has always been a farmer and his good judgment, excellent taste, and love of nature are plainly manifest in the improvements upon the Miller farm. There is none better in the country." On and on these accounts ran about their people. Wonderful things said about their people, weren't they?

"Well, Salome," Sarah looked at her younger daughter who was now in her forties, "We mustn't judge. Leave that up to the Lord. Sturdy, well-painted buildings and livestock in the pastures—they all give testimony to diligence and self-respect. God knows what's in the hearts of people. We mustn't judge."

"I think Barb would have liked to have our place described in that book, Mother. She takes such pride in it."

Just then, one of Barb Yoder's magnificent green-blue, iridescent peacocks called out in its warbling, piercing cry from the highest point above the north roof rim of the huge barn. Swiss barn, they called it. Barb Yoder did take pride in her place. Right now she was deep in the woods over there by Camp Branch filling her milk buckets with those huge blackberries that grew by the creek.

Barb Yoder had gradually taken over leadership of the farm. It was she who designed the new wing on the house and the extensive upstairs. They had eleven rooms now, including the new bathroom upstairs with real hot and cold water in the wintertime.

They still had the privy out there by the garden and plum

trees. Couldn't go that far yet. After all, too many changes make one's head swim. And here it was the turn of the century. There were so many changes, a body couldn't keep up.

Those heavy steam registers had been something else though. Had to get several strong neighbor men to help the plumber get it all hooked up. When the gigantic furnace was fired up that first time and she twisted the valves open on those registers awaiting the hot steam that hissed and seeped through the pipes, she had been in joyous ecstasy.

Central heating. Five bedrooms. A parlor with a bay window, south exposure. Three of the doors had those graceful, white etched glass panes in them. "Fleur-de-lis" they called the design. Well, plain as the rest of the giant farmhouse was, a touch of "fleur-de-lis" probably wouldn't get them in trouble with the bishop. Barb Yoder had to come to grips with her own pride. Decided not to have her place described in that county history book. It was a sacrifice, perhaps, but one that was right for her.

Besides, she did have a twinge of guilt over her flock of peacocks. Extravagant, some folks called them. But she kept to her plain dress, her black bonnet, her covering. They butchered meat from the fowl and livestock of the farm. They ate fruit raised right over there in the orchard. The basement shelves were filled with fruit and vegetables canned from their orchard and garden. Could allow for something beautiful, couldn't one?

Weren't they plain folks in their "plain church"? Everybody has a need for something beautiful somewhere. Besides, her place was off the main road.

Too bad the township decided not to cut the road on through over there to hook up with that nice road going to Gunn City. But, too expensive, they'd said. All those woods, two creeks to build bridges over. Their farm remained quiet, isolated, off the main road. Let her peacocks scream and holler. They bothered no one as they roamed widely through her orchard, lawn, and barnyard. Pastoral and peaceful, that's what it was.

Barb's stained fingers gently lifted the blackberries from their holdings on the tall, thorny spikes. Her sunbonnet shielded her forehead from the scalding sun.

Barb's mind worked best as she picked. She thought about their life together, how the Lord had led them through thick and thin. My, how the time flies. Why, she'd come to this county as a little girl after the Civil War. Her sister Nancy, a child of the Border Wars, was long dead, buried beneath a towering, sweeping pine tree in the East Cemetery over west by Harrisonville.

Noah, her brother, was getting older, too. Her nephews, Seth and Simon? Well, they were young men now. Seth had been eyeing one of those Model T Fords he'd seen down at Garden City when he and Salome and she had sold hickory nuts from the back of the spring wagon years ago. Whew! Barbara Yoder didn't know if she'd be able to keep up with things at this pace.

Then there were her nieces, Mary Barbara, named after her, and that wiry, fun-loving Twili who'd come along five years after Mary Barb. Why, they were getting to be a family, weren't they, in spite of the fact that she and Salome had not married?

It used to bother Salome a lot, but she, Barbara, was long used to her single state. There were blessings in not having to be accountable to a man. Wasn't one of her favorite verses that one her mother liked: "There is neither Jew nor Greek, male nor female." If ever there was a Bible verse that leveled folks out, that was it. She'd ponder that one again when she had time.

Yes, she had a family, the three of them. Didn't they work well together? Where one left off the other took up. God knows what's best. Why they worked as well together as those three women picking up the wheat in that picture called "The Gleaners" hanging over her leather and oak couch. She'd bought the picture at the sale in Garden City. If Mr. B.V. Vandenberg, the banker, called it art and had it hanging in his living room, guess she could have some real art in her living room too, hanging there across from her bay window.

Barb was thankful that she hadn't run across many snakes today. She hated those big black snakes that surprised one suddenly in the blackberry patch. She'd been startled by a medium-sized blue racer while she was coming down the path this morning by those hickories.

She almost threw her berry pails over her head when the thing raced towards her a mile a minute, slithering and twisting. Straight at her. It petrified her at first; she just couldn't move a muscle. "Surely this snake's not gonna run over my shoe and up my stocking?" she thought, in panic. Just as her throat constricted to let out a war whoop, that frightened blue racer darted headfirst down a hole three inches in front of her shoe. She'd had to sit on a log awhile to calm her beating heart and get her breath back.

What did one expect out in nature like this? God made the snakes too. Only thing was that since they'd put in that furnace and hot water system, they'd had to run all those long pipes through those joists in the basement ceiling. She'd never seen a snake in the basement. Barb Yoder always looked up and around first, before proceeding very far in that basement, though.

Twice she'd found six-foot-long snakeskins entangled over those water pipes. They'd come in, that's for sure. Salome might pass out if she walked under those pipes on her way to the potato bin and she saw a big black snake hanging on them. Barb? Well, she wouldn't pass out, but she'd probably wake up the dead in the cemetery over there by Clearfork.

Her milk pails full of the glistening blackberries, Barb Yoder headed along the path toward the hill. She stopped by that little spring coming out of some rocks at the edge of the creek. Setting her buckets down, she threw back her sunbonnet, bent over, and dipped the cool water up over her sweaty brow.

Yes, she thought, this was a good place, a beautiful place. Father and Mother made the right choice after the war, moving back over here. If she'd been living on that plot of land way over there by Grand River, she'd be out of the community of her people. It was so much better this way with people of their faith all around her. All you had to do was to look at the county plot map to see it. She did take a little pride in seeing their farm marked as "The Yoder Sisters' Farm."

She wouldn't brag, of course, but she was somebody, wasn't she?

Chapter 30

Refreshed by the rest and the cool spring water, Barb picked up her berries and started for the path up the hill leading home. She tipped her body sideways on the path to keep her shoulder free of the patch of pawpaw trees, shaking their giant tobacco- like leaves in the wind.

Salome couldn't stand them. "Gag a buzzard," she'd said, spitting out the pulp and pretty brown seeds. But she, Barb, liked pawpaws. Why the way they looked, there'd be lots of pawpaws with their musky, heady aroma for a pie, come September. Going to be a bumper crop of hickory nuts, too. Her mind wandered.

When she arrived at the barnyard gate, sweat soaking through the back of her dress, her heart lifted. There came her sister-in-law, Nettie Yoder, with her daughters, Mary Barb and Twili.

"Auntie Barb! Auntie Barb!" The girls raced towards her joyfully. "Let us help! Let us help!" The girls grabbed the berry-filled pails from their tired aunt.

"Gotta' tell you what happened, Aunt Barb, last night. Didn't get a spankin' either." Then both girls broke down in giggles. "You tell it, Twili, you do it better," said Mary Barb.

"Well, Mary Barb is always bragging about how she can whirl things around over her head. Calls it, cent—, cent—. What do you call it, Mary Barb?"

"Centrifugal force, silly." Then both girls bent over in hysterics.

"Well, Mary Barb showed me how to swing a bucket of milk around with my arm that way, way over my head, over and over again. Guess what, never spilled a drop. Ever try it, Aunt Barb?"

As a matter-of-fact, both Salome and she had tried it. So had their brother Noah in his time. "Well, yes, I believe we youngsters all did that in our day. Never spilled a drop of milk either."

"Well, last night—," Twili burst into laughter again, "last night as I was coming out of the henhouse with a milk pail full of eggs, Mary Barb said, 'Here, let me have that.'" Then, Twili sat down with the pail of blackberries between her shoes and knees as laughter shook her.

"I said, no. Mother wouldn't want us to play with the eggs. 'Give me that pail,' said Mary Barb. So I let her have it. 'Gonna show you what I can do with a pail full of eggs.' Well, she showed us both. Oh!" Then both girls shook and roared in their hysterical laughter.

"Auntie Barb, you oughta' seen Mary Barb. Me, too. Mary Barb gave that pail of eggs a big swing and when it got up over her head, all the eggs let loose. All of them." The laughter overcame them all, Barb Yoder, too, as she could see in her mind her two frolicking nieces sporting around.

"All the eggs broke. Every one of them. You should have seen our hair, our dresses. Egg yolk dripping off our noses. Yuck!"

"Your mother probably locked you both in the basement or the smokehouse, didn't she?" Barbara Yoder appreciated a good prank, a good story. This was a bit much, though, and had the times not been so prosperous, it could have been a painful tragedy.

"We didn't lie," said Twili, sobering, as she remembered her mother's face with "What happened to you girls?" written all over it.

"We told her we broke the eggs. Took the blame for it. We felt awful, and wanted to crawl under the bed. But Mother was nice about it. She even laughed and said, 'Well, don't you girls know egg shampoo is the best thing for your hair?'" Then Twili shook again with laughter.

Now this was life. Real life—the fun of it, the tricks and pranks of it, the surprises of it. Children, girls, boys, hard times, good times. Births and birthday cakes, sickness, death and funerals, all of it. Family, people of God, all of them in a community. A white meetinghouse calling them to prayer and worship when they were soul weary and when they needed to jointly give praise and thanks.

Noah's wife, Nettie, had a solemn, dignified air about her. Plainer than most of the women her age, it was all right if Noah and Nettie kept themselves according to the plain ways.

Nettie's covering strings blew in the wind as she reached out her hand to take one of the pails of berries.

"Oh, Barb, you know where the best of all the berries grow. I must come and pick with you. Would you have time next week?"

"Can't wait that long, Nettie, but come back on Friday and I'll go down over the creek by the railroad tracks with you. Bigger berries than these growing there." Barb loved Noah's wife. Nettie knew just how to put others first. Barb couldn't remember when she'd ever heard Nettie Yoder speak unkindly about anyone. No matter what a person did, Nettie always tried to understand. Wouldn't she have made a good deacon or preacher? Why, Nettie Yoder could teach a Sunday school class so's no one went to sleep, ever, and that's more'n one could say about some preachers she knew.

"It's a while yet before chores and suppertime. Why not wash off a few of these big blackberries and all of us have a taste?" Barb, putting on her apron, hastened to the water bucket to get some cold water to rinse the berries. "Salome, could you get the cream from the well?"

What a treat to eat blackberries right out of the patch doused with cold, fresh cream drawn up from the well. Salome too made her contribution, cutting slices from the yellow cake she'd taken out of the oven in the summer kitchen that noon. Fresh cake—laden with butter, spices, and sugar—cream, and berries made a good snack for the afternoon. Their spoons clanked on the ironstone bowls. "Don't get those berries on the front of your dresses, girls," warned Salome.

"Have to send you home with a chunk of my lye soap to get it out," added Sarah, who sat in the kitchen rocker spooning in the glistening berries and cream.

They talked about folks in the growing community. They had two churches, well-filled, and folks were still moving in.

Farms of their people were strung out from way up there at Germantown School, north of East Lynne: Eli Beiler, W.S. Miller, John Kenagy, J.S. Yoder, then the Yoder Sisters' farm, followed by Elizabeth Kenagy, John Miller and L.E. Yoder and all of those Hostetlers, south of East Lynne. The big farm of Joseph Hartzler loomed up from the map; on and on the names went. Their people came from Ohio, Pennsylvania, Michigan, Indiana, Illinois, Kansas, and Nebraska, on and on.

If you turned west past East Lynne, you stumbled over the names of Adam Yoder, Amos Hartzler, Isaac King. South of East Lynne loomed farms of D. Hershberger, Sam Yoder, C.D. Yoder, M. Schrock, N.W. Yoder, on and on. Over by Clearfork other names loomed up, I.J. Plank, Dave Yoder, G. Hartzler, J.C. King, John Oesch, on and on.

When you got to Garden City, the names continued; Schrocks, all kinds of Schrocks, Helmuths, and Kauffmans.

What kind of miffed Sarah, there in her chair, spooning up the last of her cream and berries, was that whoever put those names on that plot map only mentioned the men's names, except "The Yoder Sisters," meaning her two, Salome and Barb, and that other woman, Elizabeth Kenagy.

Well, she was proud about that, she was. What was that

Bible verse, "There is neither male nor female." If she'd have her way, she'd see to it that that plot map said "Rudolph and Mary Yoder," and so forth, that's what she'd do.

Nettie Yoder filled them in on the news about how she was getting along with her log cabin quilt. The girls were pitching in and learning to quilt. "That Mary Barb, why, she's going to be as good a quilter as her own Aunt Barb."

Nettie smiled, her face filled with tenderness and love. Here she'd come to see if she and the girls could help out with the canning and if she wasn't being sent home with a whole bucket full of Barb's blackberries and a hunk of Grandma Sarah's cheese.

Sarah still followed the old recipe she'd used way back during the Civil War. Still used that cheese ring with those holes punched in it, made by Solomon, before he got caught up in the war. She and Nancy used to make this cheese together. They'd savor each bite.

Soon Nettie and her daughters climbed into their buggy and bid warm farewells. "See you all at church, come Sunday." They waved, and then they galloped off. Sarah Yoder hoped that the time would never come when family members would cease to say, "I'll see you in church, come Sunday."

As the buggy wheels turned in the soft brown earth, Twili and Mary Barb leaned out and called back. "We forgot our poem, Grandma, Aunties. We forgot our poem. Stop, mother."

Kindhearted Nettie Yoder halted her horse while the smiling girls leaned out of the buggy to chant in unison the poem they'd memorized about Ivory Soap. Without a giggle, too.

> Don't thee wed for money, friend;
> For money hath a sting,
> Don't thee wed a pretty face;
> 'Tis but a foolish thing;

Don't thee wed for place nor fame;
'Twill disappoint your hope.
But when thee marries, choose a girl
Who uses Ivory Soap.

Salome and Barb Yoder waved as the buggy with their giggling nieces picked up speed. They allowed as how they were in perfect harmony with that Ivory Soap poem, although they never used the soap themselves.

Chapter 31

Theodore Roosevelt was up there in the White House in Washington, D.C., taking over the managing of the country. Could say things were going along according to par, if you overlooked that depression of '93.

Out here in the Midwest everyone read about Mary Elizabeth Leace over in Kansas urging her citizens to "Raise less corn and more hell." Terrible thing to say, thought Barb Yoder.

Hordes of immigrants kept coming into the country, continuing their spread through the big eastern cities and across the westward plains. If you picked up a magazine or paper, chances are you'd read an advertisement or catchy slogan about something to buy. Well, out here in the Mennonite community, folks taught their youngsters to ignore such advertisements. Still, they thumbed through the pages of the magazines reading the enticing ads. "Ponds Extract—Relief for every pain. Drink Hires Root Beer! Take Scotts Emulsion for assimilation." Little Simon Yoder, Seth's son, didn't rightly know what "assimilation" meant and kept pestering his mother, Nettie, about it.

Two of the older Oesch boys over by Garden City had tried their luck smoking those Panama cigars, spread out on a half-page advertisement. Go into a drug store, chances are you'd see a funny sign about those cigars and cigarettes:

"Cigarette smoke, like lighted punk, Hath a fetid stink, like a lively skunk!"

Then too, these Mennonite girls eyed the dresses they saw in *Harpers Bazaar,* all spread out in store windows: tight waist, high neck, puffed sleeves, and tiered skirts. They were taught to keep their dresses simple and plain, but once in awhile one of those puffed-sleeve dresses showed up on a Mennonite girl in a photograph taken over at Bowman's Studio in Harrisonville.

No tiered skirts, though. They had to draw a line somewhere. Locked in forever on pasteboard, for the whole world to see. A Mennonite girl sitting for a picture with puffed sleeves on her dress. Well, I'm sure the deacon, preachers, and the bishop over at both of those large Mennonite churches had more than a few words to say about that from time to time.

Salome and Barb Yoder were outside looking over their pigs, allowing as how they would soon be ready for market. Then Salome checked her notes in that little calendar book she held in her hand. The big guernsey, Beulah, would be having her calf next month.

Turning their worn shoes in the fine barnyard dust, Barb thought she heard a cry, or was it just one of the guinea fowl letting out a morning squawk? Then, Salome turned. "Mother! I think I hear Mother calling."

They ran as fast as they could. Salome held her book with the animal husbandry information tightly to her bosom. Barb's sunbonnet blew off in her haste. She did not bother to turn aside to snatch it up as they headed past the corncrib, up the grade, past the buggy style, and onto the sidewalk that ran past the milk house. Salome's feet hit the porch first.

"Mother, you called?" she shouted, opening the screen door.

Sarah wasn't in the dining room, nor in the kitchen. Was she in the pantry back toward the garden? Barb and Salome couldn't find her there either. Then they noticed the open door leading down to the basement.

Oh no! Sarah Yoder, their mother didn't go down those steps, did she? Why, she had been feeling poorly these past two months. They'd had the doctor over at East Lynne have a look at her, but he only prescribed Hagworth's Tonic. Far as she could see the Hagworth's Tonic hadn't braced her up one bit. Took a nip of it herself and found it tasted just like that bottle of bourbon that Simon Zook kept hidden in that little spot above the cow feeding troughs when he came over in the winter to help. Must have much of the same ingredients.

Worried, the sisters peered down the dark steps—fifteen in all, for it was a deep basement, cold and dark.

"Mother, are you down there?" they called together. Silence. "Mother," they called again. This time there was a bit of fear in their voices. They descended on the two-inch thick steps, hand-sawed by their father soon after the Civil War.

They found Sarah crumpled on the cold cement at the bottom of the steps. Unconscious, she still held an enameled basin in her hand. Potatoes. Yes, she loved fried potatoes for noon lunch. She was on her way to the potato bin. What had happened?"

Sarah was picked up off the cement floor by her two daughters that bright day. In a few hours she rallied to consciousness and stared up at Salome and Barb. Barb's hand held a cool cloth to Sarah's forehead.

"Wh— Wh— what happened?" Sarah breathed the words slowly, her dark eyes piercing through the haze surrounding her field of vision.

"Mother, you fell. Don't seem to have any broken bones. Salome rang the dinner bell. Neighbors, including Noah, are on the way over here. We're going to send up to East Lynne for the doctor. Rest now, don't strain yourself."

Hearing the clanging dinner bell, the neighbors came. First to arrive was Emmie Eicher with a basket of her herbs and teas, including a flask of her homemade wine. The wine was for the sick and faltering, especially among the elderly.

Wasn't Sarah Yoder the oldest member of their congregation? All of those old pioneer types who'd lived through the troubles of the Civil War, they lay sleeping there with Uncle C.P. and his two wives over in the Clearfork Cemetery. End of an era if Sarah Yoder dies, they thought.

Doctor Sweeney rode out in his new Model T Ford. Maybe his knowledge of medicine was a notch better than that of the Civil War doctor to whom Sarah had taken her husband, Solomon, so many years ago.

Doctor Sweeney listened to Sarah's lungs and heart with one of those new stethoscopes, and felt her weak pulse in her fragile, tired old arm. Turning to Barb and Salome, he said, "She's tired. She suffered a stroke on the way down the steps. She still moves, but you see how she wants to sleep. Keep her quiet. I'll come out every day until she's better. I'm sorry, there's nothing more I can do. Let her rest."

Over the next few days, Sarah gained consciousness once in awhile. They placed her in the old familiar bedroom she'd long since shared with Solomon. Here, Sarah, a woman of the Border Wars, looked out past the swaying cedar trees to the towering red barn.

Leaning over, Barb caught Sarah's whisper. "Solomon ought to be coming around the bend. See that he has help with his horses."

Her smile was of sweetness, the sweetness of love, never lost, treasured in the heart. Then she fell asleep.

Sarah died five days after her fall. No daughters on earth could have better cared for her than Salome and Barb Yoder. Sarah died where she had lived, on her farm.

Since Noah would be coming by the church, Barb depended upon her brother to bring in those wooden folding chairs. Good thing Salome and she had worked hard getting those rag strips sewn together and sent up to Harrisonville to be woven into a rag carpet.

It'd taken them all summer to cut the big roll in strips,

bind the edges, then get it tacked down over a layer of straw. But, the beauty of it, the softness of it; if they had to have a funeral, let it begin right here in their front room with those blue-grey rag carpets softening things.

Before the church members and friends began to arrive with their dishes laden with food for after the funeral, Barb took time to put on her sunbonnet and take a stroll out through the pasture and into the woods. Here, she'd take time to review their lives together, take time to understand what it all meant.

When her foot scraped the rocks in that little gully where the black shale and coal showed itself from Mother Earth, she thought of how life really was. Rocky places, hard places. Dark places too, dark as the bottom of the well.

She opened the weathered gate by the woods and sauntered on, toward those tall, white spikes of wild delphinium growing by the green gooseberry bushes.

Yes, life provided flowers and green growing things. Why, her mother used to tell her how the flowers grew in that little patch of woods by Grand River over by Harrisonville where she and her father first lived in this new country. Violets, May Apples, Dutchman's Breeches, the beautiful showy Evening Primroses that lined the dirt roads hereabouts—they softened the dark and hard places in life. Well, she thought to herself, like that wise man said in the Bible, everything has its time and season.

Her right shoe caught the edge of a rotted log, throwing her sideways. Barb caught herself. She cried now, freely the tears ran. How different life would be without her mother. It's God's will, isn't it? Beginnings and endings.

Even the white wild delphiniums blooming around her feet had a beginning and an ending. I guess what really matters, she thought, was how we bloom, how we live, to what we commit ourselves.

Sarah King Yoder had committed herself to marriage, to

motherhood, to building this farm—hour by hour, toil upon toil. And the church—the meetinghouse, the Bible, the songs. How Sarah loved to sing the songs of faith.

And, no place was so special, so sacred, as the meetinghouse where she sat on Sunday, surrounded by the people of her faith, good people, hardworking people, who joined with her to build a community. Church and community. Can't have one without the other.

Chapter 32

Barb was glad Salome and she had taken time to look through their mother's worn Bible. There it was, Psalm 23: "The Lord is my shepherd, I shall not want." Brother Levi Miller would be speaking on this psalm at the service in their home.

They found a small, folded piece of paper that looked old, very old, with some handwriting on the back. It looked like their father, Solomon's, handwriting. What caught their attention, though, was that verse their mother had copied down: "There is neither Jew nor Greek, there is neither bond nor free, there is neither male nor female: for ye are all one in Christ Jesus."

Barb freshened herself in the washroom, wiping her face with a cool cloth. She didn't take much time with mirrors, but now she studied her face in the small nine-by-twelve-inch mirror. Her people didn't hold to copious standing and primping in front of mirrors. "Fifty. Half a century."

The thoughts continued. "Giving my time and strength to home, this home, this land, this family. No, never married, but neither did Salome. Bothered Salome more than it did her, didn't it? Well, she wasn't finished yet. Got a farm to run. Twentieth century, wasn't it, with that Roosevelt up in Washington, the one who liked to shoot those grizzly bears out west?

Guess she had plenty of juice left in her to carry her on ahead. With all the fast changes sweeping through the community, she might not be able to keep up with it all, but she would sure give it a try.

Undertaker Eberly had brought Sarah Yoder's embalmed body back to the home yesterday afternoon. The simple, grey, cloth-covered casket rested quietly there in the living room across from the bay window. They'd had to move the oak library table from the center of the room. Yes, the grey of the casket fitted perfectly above the new blue rag carpets beneath.

Neither Salome nor Barb, grieving the loss though they were, had been too overcome by the family gathering last night. Fitting, wasn't it? Family all together before a casket. Mother in the casket, too. A work-worn mother. Look at her face, pale in death, wrinkled like fine old parchment. The tender smile on her closed lips hinted at what her closed eyes may have seen when her spirit left her body. Who greeted her from the other side? Solomon? Nancy? her own mother and father?

Or was it the very face of the blessed Jesus who stretched out his hand and helped her across Jordan? Then, Barb Yoder remembered the old stories of a slave woman who had lived with her mother and her sister Nancy so long ago.

That was when the winds of war—a most awful, burning, killing war—blew over their home. She remembered her mother singing and humming some of those heartrending songs that old slave woman, Marianne, had taught her. What was it? "I tole Jesus it'd be all right if he changed my name."

Tears began to stream down Barb's face as she strode into the bedroom to lift her prayer covering from its mount on the carnival glass vase. She was glad she had a new, crisp, white covering. New strings on it, too. She checked her hair, parted in the middle, drawn tightly into a bun in the back. Fitting the covering on over her grey hair, covering strings falling down below her chin and on to the shoulders of her black crepe dress, she surveyed herself.

Not old. Fiftyish, yes. Still trim and solid. Hard work and diligence to the daily commitments kept her body healthy. Guess there was a lot of life in her yet. She checked the cedar chest. Her new bonnet was perched there.

Both she and Salome had ordered new bonnets out of that catalog from that big Mennonite community in Ohio. Times change. She and Salome had put their old bonnets in that ancient wooden chest in the back bedroom upstairs with all sorts of other old things like German books and Bibles.

These new bonnets suited her and Salome just fine. Plain and servicable. Let the old women wear those big bonnets with brims that came out over the forehead. As for her, this one that drew on over the back of her head suited her just fine. It covered her hair neatly, extending almost to the top of her forehead, but allowed a little of her grey hair to show.

And Salome? Well, Salome had ordered a bit of black lace which she added to the brim, just back of her forehead. They held to the plain ways: black stockings and shoes, black bonnets, black crepe dresses. They were ready for a funeral.

Even though they knew family and sisters and brothers of the church would be bringing in bountiful amounts of food, she and Salome had prepared their best ham. Barb had taken it out of the cast-iron oven this morning and sliced the savory, smoked ham into generous slices.

Salome had baked seven loaves of bread. Said it gave her something to do. Salome didn't like waiting around, and with a funeral there was this waiting—moment-by-moment, step-by-step, living through each second, each duty, each emotion.

They gathered, somberly and quietly at first. Then the life began to burst through, the life that overshadows death. Nettie and Noah came first, then came Seth and his girlfriend, Sonya Hershberger.

Mary Barb, a dutiful niece, quietly walked over to her aunts and brushed their cheeks with a kiss. My, how that Mary Barb was growing up. Full-bosomed, hair put up under her covering—no wonder that Ike Miller kept staring at her like he did. Well, more on that later.

Niece Twili sat demurely there in the living room after she'd again taken a long look at her grandmother, resting peacefully. Twili, at fourteen, was a quiet girl. Barb knew she'd want to talk about all this later.

And nephew Simon? Well, Simon, with his shoot of orange hair sticking up in the back, was taking it all in. She knew Simon was figuring out the religious and spiritual meaning of all of this, which was fitting for a Christian youth who had been baptized with that group of twenty-five last fall. Simon was a thinker, a sensitive lad. He could explain the Bible well, too. He'd probably be a preacher someday.

One thing was for certain: Simon Yoder would soak up every aspect of these services today. He would be quoting the Bible verses to himself tomorrow, going over it all in his mind. Simon Yoder never was tempted to carve his initials in the church bench; he was far too sensitive and too overwhelmed by the gracious things of worship and faith to let his mind wander like Seth's did that time.

Neighbors came, too, those close by. Barb knew that the church would be full, come one o'clock. After they'd all taken a look at old Sarah Yoder's pale body stretched out in death, they spoke comforting words to Salome and Barbara.

Some shed tears, for it was a great loss. Who in their community knew what Sarah Yoder knew? Who could remember such events, such leading of the hand of God through the Civil War times and through the settling of this community? Who would carry on her simple faith? Today they would bury a woman who had never given in to self-pity and despair. Somehow, with God's help, Sarah had triumphed over the hardships and pains of life.

Preacher Miller began the service. Every downstairs room was filled with people, members of the church as well as a few of the nearest English neighbors.

"We are gathered here to remember our departed sister, Sarah Yoder, and to look to the Christ who led her so faithfully through the years." His voice shook a little, as his own grief at this loss took hold of him. "Our sister left this passage marked in her Bible. It is a good passage, a passage everyone here should take note of and live by. It is from Psalm ninety, verse twelve: 'So teach us to number our days so that we may apply our hearts unto wisdom.'"

Preacher Miller made it just fine through his short message. But when the singing began, he drew a great white handkerchief from his hip pocket, wiped tears, and blew his nose with a loud, trumpeting sound.

The song, "My Saviour First of All," was one of Sarah's favorites. Together, men and women, children included, they lifted up their voices in harmony, singing of the end of life's work and crossing the swelling tide to be greeted first of all by a smiling Savior.

> I shall know him, I shall know him,
> And redeem'd by his side I shall stand,
> I shall know him, I shall know him
> By the prints of the nails in his hand.

Salome bent over, her white covering catching in a sunbeam as she wiped the flowing tears. Barb Yoder wiped away the flowing tears, too. Silently. Softly. It would be inappropriate to wail loudly and carry on after they had just sung about such a precious hope.

Everything and everyone has a beginning and an end. Happy and blessed is the one who walks with Christ every step of the journey of life. Sarah Yoder had done that—gladly, joyously. It was fitting that she should recognize her Savior and that he should be the first to extend his nail-pierced hand to welcome her home.

After the bountiful meal, they climbed into their spring

wagons and buggies. Following the horse-drawn hearse, they headed down the treelined lane to the open road beyond. How the thick dust of the earth mellowed and softened the harshness of such a journey.

The snorts and harness sounds from the jogging horses mingled with the calls of the meadowlarks and the red-winged blackbirds swooping down from the blue sky. The countryside seemed to soften in the shadow of those billowing, windswept clouds.

Salome, next to Barb in the back seat of Seth's carriage, knew she could live through this day, for even the flowers along the wayside dipped and nodded toward her, whispering: "The grass withereth, the flower fadeth; but the word of our God shall stand forever."

Little did Salome Yoder, sitting there in her black crepe dress, head crowned with her new black bonnet tied under her chin, know what would soon come her way.

It was not a harsh, lonely ride, this funeral procession, surrounded this way by the gentleness of Mother Nature in late May. The sweet smell of honeysuckle in full bloom swept over the swaying riders, and the morning primroses in full white, nodded greetings and blessings to these dark-robed mourners.

Sarah's obituary and funeral account was printed in that famous Amish-Mennonite publication from Ohio, *The Budget:* "It is estimated that there were over one thousand people there, and two hundred teams.

"The bishop, preaching the sermon at the meetinghouse graced by those sighing sycamores, built his sermon from that most blessed of all passages for the Christian that was so fitting for the faithful life of Sarah Yoder. 'The Lord is my shepherd, I shall not want....'"

When in her life all failed and darkness prevailed, it was in these times that Sarah had been led by her Shepherd.

Marianne, the slave woman, knew this, for how to trust the loving hand of Christ was written in her heart. Do not look for the Christian life to lead to riches and to ease.

Remember that often there are rocks and thorns for the sheep to go through before they are led to the still waters. It was the loving grace of God that prepared a table before Sarah Yoder after she had supped from the bitter dregs of war, death, and near famine. Now, she could sit with her Savior, face-to-face.

The cemetery on that hill with the cedar trees was not frightening at all. The grass blew in the wind, the cedars sighed, primroses and violets blossomed freely, gracing the air. And, there too, faithful farmer hands, holding the funeral tools of the hour—the spade and pick—lifted the dark, moist earth and prepared a place for the grey casket. Human hands dug the grave—calloused hands, hands that held wives and children in love and tenderness, hands that were lifted up to God in prayer, hands that held the weary tools of toil.

Among the murmured blessings and tears of those who loved her, Sarah Yoder's body was lowered by these kind and calloused farmers' hands into the darkness of that Missouri soil. Missouri—the name the wind had whispered in her ear so long ago when her feet, with Solomon's, first touched this verdant land. Her body returned to the earth; her soul returned to the God who gave it.

Chapter 33

The deep winter mud sucked at Barb Yoder's ankles. Barb leaned against the southeasterly wind which blew a cold rain, pelting her face. She staggered toward the milk house, lit by the golden glow of two lanterns. She had the collar of her work coat turned up, still the cold water dripped from her chin and ran down into her neck. With her shoulder, she heaved the door open, setting down the two heavy milk pails, brimful.

Silently, Salome, wrapped warmly in her heavy wool sweater with her kerchief tied under her chin, draped cheesecloth over the pail. Lifting it, she emptied it into the big metal bowl of their new cream separator.

Her job was to crank the cream separator, then empty the cream into the five-gallon can, except the pint they would take inside for their cooking. The buckets of skim milk would be taken out by Barb and the hired hand, Abram Zook, to bucket feed the two small calves.

They never talked much together, these sisters, early in the morning. It was better this way. They needed to get the chores done. God knew what they had planned to do today. And, they'd been doing it now for the past two weeks.

Sickness had broken out in the community, dreadful sicknesses—typhoid fever and smallpox. Diligence and a commitment to their people drove them, these sisters, as well as many others within the congregation. Volunteer hands and hearts were needed when infants and children as well as adults around them were flattened by pestilence.

They'd been volunteering, Salome and Barb. Little time for extras, no time for baking pie or cake. Stir up some cornmeal mush, stew some beans with a chunk of pork thrown in. Why should a Christian waste time with fine recipes when folks from the congregation were dying around them?

No, there was no time for prolonged finery now. As soon as they finished these chores, they would have a bite of that scrapple on the back of the kitchen range and a cup of coffee. Then they'd bundle up that bread baked last evening, along with slices of the smoked shoulders and hams, a few jars of their canned sausage and canned green beans, plus those night garments made of warm flannel they'd hurriedly stitched up on their foot pedaled sewing machine, and off they'd trot to Mose Lehman's place where his wife, Esther, lay in bed with smallpox.

Barb took a couple of comforters they'd just finished, rolled them up, and tossed them there on the back seat of the surrey.

They'd hitched both horses, Timmon and Hank, to the surrey since the mud and clay were so thick this time of the year. They only hoped they'd make it without having to get out and find a loose fence post to poke the mud out of the spokes.

The cold rain continued, blowing down into the surrey as if to blast them out and let misfortune reign. With grim faces they toiled along, Timmon and Hank laboring, steam floating back from their wide open nostrils. Barb yanked the reins, turning the team from the uphill grade out of the long lane up onto the wide road leading up to Smith Schoolhouse.

"Oh mercy!" she thought, "There comes old man Stoner down the hill in his Model T truck. God help us." The truck swayed and lurched back and forth across the clay hill, dangerously avoiding the deep side ditches.

Stoner, their neighbor down the way, headed toward them, leaning into the mud-splashed windshield of his Ford, gripping the wooden wheel with his massive hands, as if to escape the gates of perdition. Fortified too, he was, with his own two-year-old apple jack, just like that old timer Mack Sherman, Sarah'd told them about. On he came. Mud and water splashed.

"Pull over, Barb! Pull over!" The fear in Salome's voice caught in the wind of the open surrey, mingling with the fog and dreary rain. Behind them they heard the lonesome lament of the Rock Island train, wailing as if it were lost in the storm and winter fog.

Again Barb yanked her team, getting the surrey wheels out of the deep ruts in the road and over to the sloping shoulder. She didn't want her surrey going sideways down into that ditch like Samantha Troyer's did last summer on this hill. Then, old Timmon, the nervous horse, rose up in terror at the approaching Ford. "Get out and hold the bridle, Salome, get out and hold his bridle!"

Salome obeyed, silently sliding off the leather seat into the seemingly bottomless mud. She didn't take the time to notice how the cold water and mud from the ruts squashed up over the tops of her galoshes.

"Whoa, Timmon, whoa!" She held his bridle, patting and comforting him as the steaming Model T truck blundered toward them. Salome, in disgust at the whole affair, turned her back on old man Stoner. Let Barb bid him "how-de-do" on this fine day if she pleased, and yes, next time, if she pleased, let her get out and drench her ankles in this freezing mud and water.

Barb knew Salome was put out at her. But she nodded and tried to smile at Stoner, twisting and putt-putting by in his Ford. Probably be in the ditch before he got to his lane. Besides, he was so intent on staying out of the ditch right now that she doubted he even noticed her.

On they went, three more miles. Salome was so silent. She had been this way ever since they'd been coming over here to help Mose Lehman with his smallpox-stricken wife, Esther. Salome, with her more delicate constitution, paled at the sight of such sickness: awful boils and steamy pustules, fever-glazed eyes, parched lips, and looks of absolute terror on their faces.

Well, it took the steam out of you, Barb did admit it. And that Model T they'd just passed, wouldn't mind driving one of those Fords herself one day. Why was she putting it off? Well, when they got home this afternoon, she'd give it some more thought. Certain, Barb was, that she'd keep her Ford straight on the road and not scare the horses and everyone else half to death like old man Stoner just did. But what was ailin' Salome, quiet and put out like she seemed?

She'd been quieter, more to herself, since they first came over to Esther Lehman's last week. Her husband, Mose, had kept the hall door and the kitchen doors closed and away from the dreaded sickroom where Esther lay, pustules erupting all over her face.

Salome'd insisted on taking that soup bone Mose had just brought in from the smokehouse. She went into the kitchen and began peeling and quartering a few potatoes to get a rich beef stew started. Barb had unfolded the ironing board and put the heavy sadirons on the kitchen range after stoking up the fire with a few sticks of that hedge wood. If you wanted a quick hot fire, shove in a stick or two of hedge wood, that's for sure.

Barb ironed and Salome kept turning and talking to Mose. Guess a body borne down by the weight of such ghastly sickness as the smallpox that'd stricken his wife needed a little visit to take his mind off of it. Enough to make a man crazy, really. His oldest daughter, Orpha, sat in that darkened room by her mother's side, doing all she could to keep her mother on this side of the grave. Strange too, she a visiting type of woman herself, Barb Yoder, just kind of set her mouth and chin and bore down on that iron as she pressed the sheets and Mose's work shirts and all those homemade underdrawers where the words "Robin Hood Flour" still showed through. Funny, Barb couldn't think of a thing to say.

"And what did the doctor say about Esther this morning?" Salome turned away from the hot kitchen range while stirring her soup to face Mose, sitting there with his black beard cascading down. It gave him a fierce and strong look. Mature man, Mose Lehman was, that's for sure.

"Well, Doctor Balter, he says poor Esther's at a mighty low point. Hardly anybody in these parts has made it, when it comes to smallpox." Mose took his red handkerchief out of his tight back overall pocket and blew his nose loudly.

"I'm praying for Esther. You too, Mose. And Orpha. So's Barb. Aren't you, Barb?" Salome turned to face Barb.

"Oh, yes, 'course we're praying for you. Bishop Hartzler had special prayer in service last week, Mose. Special prayer meeting for all those brought low with illness in our community."

But Barb noticed how alive Salome looked, her lithe forty-seven-year-old body swaying back and forth as she stirred her stew. Why, in this light one hardly noticed the grey in her hair. There was still a lot of yellow catching the sunlight.

Her face didn't wrinkle either. Salome kept better care of her complexion than Barb did. Salome always wore a big-brimmed sunbonnet or a straw hat in the summer sun, while Barb was just as happy if hers blew off and let the fresh air blow across her hot scalp. Then too, here lately Salome had insisted on buying some of that Ivory Soap. And even worse, she got herself a jar of that Ponds Face Cream. What was the world coming to? Well, Barb would keep it to herself; there was no use spreading scandal.

Salome had made Mose and Orpha a fine pot of beef stew. Poor dying Esther couldn't eat; all Orpha got down her was a few teaspoons of warm tea. Barb had the shirts and the underdrawers all ironed and folded, ready for Orpha to put away. Then she folded the freshly-ironed sheets, placing them on a kitchen chair. Yes, it was a sad time, such dreadful sickness, the fog settling down outside, casting greyness over everything; the two of them here with this Mose Lehman family.

They didn't really think about it, Barb and Salome. But they took upon themselves some of the pain and suffering of the sick ones and their brokenhearted family members as they ministered, washed, ironed, swept, cleaned, and cooked for them.

Family after family. They shared the fruits of their garden and the labors of their hands and prayers of their hearts. They did not grunt and strain and say to themselves, "We will carry out Christ's command and serve the unfortunate and the sick and dying."

No, their service was of love, a deep love that welled up within from some hidden spring. They worked and prayed not for thanks, but out of their care for others. Did not the blessed Jesus himself tell about those who labor so, forgetting themselves so, lost in caring for others through the love of Christ flowing through them and out to the sick, the lonely, the bereaved?

"Then shall the King say unto them on his right hand, Come, ye blessed of my Father, inherit the kingdom prepared for you from the foundation of the world: For I was an hungered, and ye gave me meat; I was thirsty, and ye gave me drink; I was a stranger, and ye took me in; Naked, and ye clothed me: I was sick, and ye visited me.... Then shall the righteous answer him, saying, Lord, when saw we thee an hungered, and fed thee, or thirsty, and gave thee drink? When saw we thee a stranger, and took thee in? or naked, and clothed thee? Or when saw we thee sick or in prison, and came unto thee? And the King shall answer and say unto them, Verily I say unto you, Inasmuch as ye have done it unto one of the least of these my brethren, ye have done it unto me."

Mose Lehman, eyes glistening with tears, followed them out to the surrey. Barb threw her bundles into the back seat and untied Timmon and Hank. Mose helped Salome pack her buckets and packages into the space in back, then helped her up into the buggy.

One could tell that Mose Lehman, tears glistening through his dark eyelashes like that, was truly grateful. And Salome called it to Barb's attention too, as the surrey bounced and swayed on over to Manasseh Hershbergers where three of their children lay, throats all choked full of mucus, fever burning them up.

"Never noticed how Mose Lehman had such long black eyelashes, did you, Barb?"

Well, it put Barb out this time. Barb, the thick-skinned one who hardly ever got miffed. But she tried not to show it. The only thing was, as the surrey rocked on, neither one of them said another word.

CHAPTER 34

Esther Lehman, a good-hearted woman and tender, loving mother, died the night after Salome Yoder made that beef stew. And she wasn't the only one. Two of the Hershberger children died of the diphtheria; they choked to death on that awful mucus.

So, Salome and Barb heated up their oven and baked pies and cakes for the funerals. Barb even threw in the last smoked shoulder of pork in her smokehouse; she cut it into thick slices for sandwiches.

The wind howled. Ice glazed the windows. The fog descended. Chimneys and trees stood stark and lonely, as the wind howled, blowing funeral wailings over the grey, cold land.

Only the words of their faith buoyed them through such greyness, through the sadness of opened graves, rain, and funeral mournings.

But greyness, sadness, and sickness all pass in time. Spring came. The sun rose in brilliance through the pink sky. Awakening birds sang morning prayers. The spring wind breathed a prayer of hope. Life moved on. Remember the words of the writer: "To every thing there is a season, and a time to every purpose under the sun."

That must have applied to Salome Yoder. After the wheat harvest was over that summer and the goldenrod was just beginning to bob and nod along the roadside and ditches, Mose Lehman rode over in a spanking new 1916 Chevrolet.

It didn't "putt-putt," like one of those Model T Fords. It purred and rumbled through the soft summer dust of the road. It had plush purple seats, a wooden steering wheel, and it made a body dizzy with its speed coming down the hill toward Barb and Salome's place. Mose Lehman took Salome Yoder to evening services over at the meetinghouse. They'd said Barb could come along.

"No, thank you kindly." Barb had tried to smile as she said it, but if you looked at her closely you could see hurt in her dark eyes, and her mouth was set as if she had a toothache.

So Salome rode in the new Chevrolet with Mose Lehman, the widower of the past winter, the one with the long dark eyelashes. A real man, he was. Six feet. Almost as tall as their father, Solomon Yoder. Barb wouldn't admit that he was a good-looking man. Shouldn't think of such foolish things.

While Barb went out to hitch up Timmon to her buggy, three of her peacocks flew up onto the ridge of her barn and spread their tails. What comfort and beauty they brought to her. Last week the county agent had brought three city ladies out here to see Barb Yoder's place: the Swiss barn, the fine painted buildings; the order of it all, trimmed, clipped, buildings sparkling in white and red paint. Only the peacocks mattered now. They stretched out their long blue-green necks and cried their piercing cries. Inside, Barb Yoder's heart bled. Tears flowed.

She remembered living through that grasshopper plague of 1875. She'd flogged, scraped, fought off, and burned until she nearly fell over dead. She'd made it, hadn't she?

Took the lead with the children too, Salome and Noah, picking until her fingers bled and selling those gooseberries with her mother for a nickel a gallon, let alone the endless bushels of hickory nuts they'd sold as children. There'd been drought—two years when crops didn't amount to a sick-kitten-on-a-jam-rock. That's right. Still she'd made it.

The worst thing of all, though, was how lonely she'd felt sitting on that bench with the other unmarried sisters of the church without Salome beside her. She wished too, that folks of the congregation wouldn't call them "unclaimed blessings" that way.

Salome had caught her man all right, faster than Esther Kropf caught those squabs on the rafter in her barn with her hairnet. A man—handsome one to boot—didn't ask a Mennonite woman of Salome Yoder's age to evening services unless he had fixed plans in his head.

And Salome? Well the way she let those advertisements in the *Country Gentleman* turn her head and empty her purse! Salome had no fortitude to turn him away. Barb Yoder just would not think about Mose Lehman and his big hairy body. Let alone her very own sister climbing into bed with him. Better not think about it. She'd have to get used to Salome's new ways, sitting back there with the sisters her age—married ones, that is.

Salome and Mose were married in October over at Bishop Hartzler's place. They just had standups. No crowd. No singing. Just the marriage service. "Moses Lehman, do you take this woman, Salome Yoder," and so on, and on.

The standups were Annie Holsopple and Irvin King. Who knew where that relationship was headed? Barb Yoder could get along alone on her place, thank you. But if you looked at her closely you'd see how set her jaw was and how some of the light had gone out of her eyes.

Even the wind sounds lonely, doesn't it? she thought to herself. Not at all balmy and kissing the side of the cheek, it was just making that moaning sound at the east end of the eaves of her stark, white farmhouse rising up in the late afternoon brightness.

Then her sad eyes lifted and the wrinkles in her brow tightened as she focused upon the great woods over east. The treetops glistened brilliantly, with orange and yellow leaves nodding towards her.

A walk. "I'll take a walk in the woods." She cleared her throat, saying the words out loud to herself. Her apron strings trailed behind her in the wind as her rough shoes hit the path through the barnyard gate. Ablaze with color, the trees seemed to beckon her onward.

"Blessed autumn," Barb whispered. "Oh, blessed autumn." Her work-worn shoes caught in the high dry grass, almost tripping her. Her steps faltered.

"Alone." The word slipped out like the pit of a prune spit into the palm. The sound of the "A" broke in the wind. "A-lone. A-lone."

Just as she dipped her grey head under a blackberry bower and headed down that hillside to the first little stream and glen, it seemed as if the October wind caught that word, blessed it, circled her head, and touched her brown cheeks with it.

"Alone. Alone." It didn't sound so tragic after all. Why, it was surprising how a body could get used to words and ways of living by giving them time. Guess she'd decide to give it time.

Can't make lime pickles in a day. No, takes at least two weeks. Sophie Bontrager's canned tomatoes all blew up, didn't they, because she had hurried so. Thought she'd remembered her directions and raced right through so she could go with her Uncle Aaron's to that outing in Kansas City.

"Better not hurry with this." Barb threw back the bright yellow pawpaw branches. She climbed way back into the shady hollow, deep among the golden leaves laced with brown.

They sheltered her, these glad, warm autumn leaves. There she sat, scarred shoes buried in the yellow leaves. Her calloused hand found a broken stick. She began to dig in the soft dust and rake through the fallen leaves.

"Where does the road lead now?"

"Why did I have to get sick just when Menno Bender started taking me to church those two Sunday evenings so long ago?"

"Why did Menno get off on another track with that Berta Roth when Menno and I sang so well together?" The questions came. "Why? Why?"

Barb lifted her head as she heard the faroff screech of her guinea fowl crying out at a soaring hawk. "That's what I am," she thought. "Just a hunched up old grey-and-white guinea hen scratching in the dirt."

Resting her sunburned face in her blistered hands, she stared through the pawpaw branches to the world beyond.

The wind caught the lowing of her milk cows by the barnyard gate. So what if it was milking time. Let them wait. It hurt, getting used to that word, "alone." It still felt like a lump of sour dough at the bottom of her stomach.

"Guinea hen—old guinea hen—that's all I am." She was talking out loud again as the tears ran down the lines in her brown cheeks. Still her hand dug with her stick in the dry earth.

"Menno Bender could have waited 'till I'd gotten over that scarlet fever, couldn't he?"

Oh well, this was life. Bishop Hartzler pointed out, again and again, what that preacher in Ecclesiastes said, "There is a time for everything under the sun."

Guess this was her time to turn a new page, like in her scrapbook upstairs in the bedroom. New page, fresh and clean. She could decide what she was going to put on that page, couldn't she? Well, maybe not just by herself. The Lord was known to throw down a few unforeseen things to keep it interesting and surprising.

Then, too, President Woodrow Wilson was throwing in lots of new things for folks to ponder and get used to and decide whether or not they were important enough to put in the scrapbook of their lives.

Just as the evening wind shifted the pawpaw branches, Barb Yoder heard the piercing cry of her peacocks. They were hungry. They needed her now. They waited for her calloused hand and cooing sounds and the scattering of their evening grain.

Barb rose, brushed the leaves from her dress and hair. It was her place now, wasn't it? "The Barb Yoder Place."

Her steps quickened as she climbed up the hill through the wild asters. When she got to the crown, it burst before her. Her place.

The orange sun had settled between purple clouds still flanked by billows of white and pink. Her cedars, dark and stately, tossed their branches toward her as if to say, "Come, Barb. Come Barb Yoder. We love you."

The stonework on the lower part of her towering barn looked like pure gold in the light, and the red frame of the barn rose above the gold. There on the roof, her three peacocks spread their emerald feathers. A flock of pigeons descended for the night.

Then a shaft of light pierced the azure bank of clouds; the windows of her house burst with golden light.

"My place." She breathed the words. "My place. I'm alone, but not lonely here."

Her gleaming farmhouse, set between the scarlet of her oak tree and the yellow maples, smiled from its doors and windows in the evening light.

Barb Yoder knew then that her life was far from over. She began to run. Wisps of grey hair dislodged in the wind. They needed her—her cows, her chickens, her peacocks, the land, the animals.

And her sister Salome still needed her, and Seth and Simon and Twili and Mary Barb. And, what about all of the others in the church?

Oh, yes, God was calling her and her lifeblood raced through her.

They'd turned a page, she and sister Salome, and they both could go on, for the Lord beckoned them with tasks for their hands to perform and offered them the grace to do them.

As Barb Yoder's feet led her up that little grade where the dry jimsonweed rattled in the wind, she began to chuckle. She remembered that this was the night she was going to go upstairs when the milking was finished and she'd had her supper. She was going to go upstairs, get down on her knees, dig out that little tin box from under her bed, and count those greenbacks she'd been saving for so long.

As soon as she had her 800 dollars, she decided right now, she was going to plunk it down on one of those new Model T Fords and drive it right out here to her place. Barb Yoder's Place.

THE END

Coming Soon

Barbara: Sarah's Legacy

Sequel to *Sarah of the Border Wars*

Who would have guessed that beneath those pleasantly aged features, the white prayer covering, the cape dress, and that pleasant and welcoming smile lay the heart and mind of a rebel!

At least that's what most of the elders thought. More than a few of her relatives in this tightly-knit Mennonite and Amish community thought so too.

She was certainly her mother's daughter. And while she didn't have to face the Civil War violence of the bushwhackers and jayhawkers that Sarah Yoder had, she had seen her own share of trouble. Her confrontations weren't with soldiers and bandits but with the rigid traditions and assumptions of the Cass County Mennonites.

But she was convinced that in Christ there is "no longer Jew or Greek, male and female," and she would live her life accordingly. She would continue the tradition of strength, faithfulness, and independence established by her mother. And God would be her cornerstone—no matter what "they" said!

Barbara: Sarah's Legacy

Today was Barbara's day and she was not going to let anybody spoil it. A broad smile spread over her face as her feet hit the front porch.

She strode on down to Arthur's car, which vibrated and shook in time to the rattling motor. She climbed in alongside him. Clutching her leather purse in her lap, she looked over to Arthur's tanned face. "This here lady's gonna get her a car today, Arthur. Let's get goin'! Hightail it out of here!"

It took them about an hour to reach Harrisonville. She could have taken the train, but riding like this with Arthur in his Plymouth, she could observe just how he did it, this driving. After all, there was not much to it: Keep on your side of the road. Give it gas. Step on the brake now and then. If anyone gets in your way, blast the horn. The only thing that worried her a little was letting out that clutch so it wouldn't jerk your bonnet off.

"No, thank you, Arthur, I won't need a ride home." No words sounded so special, so truthful, so welling up from within one's heart as those words. And Barbara Yoder, born on a snowy winter night during the Civil War, meant it.

* * *

AVAILABLE MARCH 1994

About the Author

As a child, James D. Yoder longed for a church and he found it among the Swiss Mennonites in Cass County, Missouri. "Mennonite women were my Bible school teachers. I will never forget the faith in their hearts, their singing voices, and the love of Christ reflected from their smiles."

Following an early period as clergy in the Mennonite Church, James continued his studies in counseling psychology. He holds B.A., B.S.Ed., and Th.B. degrees from Goshen (Indiana) College and Seminary, M.A. from Central Missouri State University, and Ph.D. from the University of Missouri, Kansas City. He is a licensed psychologist with fifteen years of university teaching and counseling experience, the last eleven at the University of Missouri, Kansas City. James founded the Kansas City Chapter of the Viktor Frankl Institute of Logotherapy.

Interested in writing at an early age, James's poems were published in the *Cass County Democrat*. His story about his experience with the Mennonites is told in *The Yoder Outsiders* (Faith and Life Press, 1988). He lectures widely on issues of spirituality in mental health and does storytelling from his life and writings. He is now working on his seventh book.

After nearly thirty years in Kansas City, James and his wife, Lonabelle (Jantzi) Yoder, continue their lives in Hesston, Kansas. They have one adult son, Michael. Their daughter, Angela, died at the age of eight.